Traditional Songs of the North of Ireland

Liam Ó Conchubhair is a singer and a teacher of songs. He has absorbed the musical heritage of the generations of traditional singers whom he has met, befriended and listened to as he travelled widely in the course of a long career in the North of Ireland. His repertoire of songs from this part of the world is second to none.

Derek Bell is a versatile classical musician and composer, though he is probably best known the world over as harpist for the traditional Irish music group, The Chieftains. His contribution to the promotion of Irish music is thus already immense, and his understanding of traditional melodies is beyond compare.

Do Mo Bhean Bheag Rua, Frances

and

for Derek's Beloved Stefanie

Traditional Songs of the North of Ireland

Liam Ó Conchubhair
&
Derek Bell

WOLFHOUND PRESS

First published 1999 by
Wolfhound Press Ltd.
68 Mountjoy Square
Dublin 1
Tel: (353-1) 874 0354
Fax: (353-1) 872 0207

British Library Cataloguing in Publication Data
A catalogue record for this book is available from the British Library

ISBN 0-86327-630-X

10 9 8 7 6 5 4 3 2 1

Cover design: Slick Fish Design, Dublin
Cover photographs: Slide File, Dublin
Book design, computer conversion & layout: Diskon Technical Services Ltd., Dublin
Printed in the Republic of Ireland by: Colour Books, Dublin

Text set in Adobe Garamond 10.5pt on 13pt

Contents

Foreword

Why this title? Why this book?

Derek Bell and I are both from Belfast, Northern Ireland. The songs were learnt and sung over the whole northern half of our country, everywhere north of a line from Blacksod Bay in Mayo to Carlingford Lough in Louth. Songs like the singing birds know no barriers in their travels. They are traditional songs, in Irish and in English, still being sung, at home and preferably well away from sound and visual media. They are vibrantly of a strong oral tradition.

The book specifies songs of the North of Ireland. Pundits have laid it down that in a country very rich in folk music, the North of Ireland is notably so. A renowned Swedish ethnomusicologist, Professor Melberg has claimed that while Ireland may stand on the same lofty pedestal in storytelling with India and Arabia, she is pre-eminent in folk-songs. Melberg estimates we have 45000 folk-songs.

I thought that my own repertoire of 200 songs, in Irish and English, was notable. But a collector in modern County Clare, Tom Munnelly has found 2000 songs on his own; and he estimates that there is a total of 6000 in Clare alone. More power to Melberg.

Until 1945 when I married, my mind was set on the Gaelic songs alone. The Gaelic songs are incomparable. But when I first came to live in the country, in County Derry, teaching in Counties Tyrone, Armagh, Antrim and Donegal, I discovered local 'bards' had emulated, perhaps unconsciously, their Gaelic forebears. *En passant* any place where Gaelic – I prefer to say Irish – was the common speech relatively recently, then the English spoken locally is often distinctive.

Introduction

Many years ago, at a concert that my band, The Chieftains, gave for the Oireachtas, I first had the pleasure of meeting Liam Ó Conchubhair. Afterwards, we talked much of Irish music; and about the problems of instrumentalists who, not knowing the Irish words of the music, could end up with the wrong tune! Liam correctly pointed out to me that, whereas Dr Paddy Moloney and The Chieftains had done much for Irish instrumental music, there are very few, if any, who have done anything comparable for the massive treasury of Irish vocal music. Still the work of Síle Ní Scolaí, the singers in Clannad, Nóirín Ní Ríain, Séan Ó Sé, Mary O Hara, Pádraigín Ní Uallacháin and her husband, Len Graham, and Maighréad Ní Dhónaill, and many others command deep respect. So far as Northern song is concerned, Liam and I both hope that this present book will greatly help to redress the balance for vocal music.

As Liam and I agreed to give concerts together, I got to know him and admire his rich voice and fine interpretation of songs. Before I met him, I felt that there were only two types of Irish singers of folk-songs:

(i) the musical ones like Ní Scolaí and the Ní Dhónaill girls who have sung with Clannad and Enya;

(ii) those with no training or technique, who sing by tightening their throat muscles, apparently actually trying to imitate the strangulated sound of the pub-singer or the drunken after-dinner ballad singer. Needless to say, Liam very much belonged to the musical type of singer. I can truthfully say that listening to him, working with him, and talking with him over the years gave me enormous pleasure.

His encyclopaedic knowledge of the Irish language, of stories and customs, of so many poets, musicians, artists and folk legends, stories and customs, and terms of speech, as well as his profound erudition in music, made it a memorable experience to spend many happy hours listening to him expound the 'Irish gospel of music'.

We not only want our singers to know our own music but we also want interested foreigners to know and love it as we do. We want our music appreciated throughout the world; but for this to occur, we must have published musical written texts of these wonderful, immortal and very beautiful songs. Otherwise, they will remain a closed book to many millions who would be interested.

Hence the timely importance of Liam's book is obvious. Throughout the many years I have known Liam I cannot count the occasions on which he has performed, with and for me, songs which but for him would be lost now and which I would certainly never have heard!

Many of these are in this book, which makes a real living and varied contribution to our musical culture. I am delighted that this great musical legacy is now published and available for all to study and perform.

May many more volumes follow.

Derek Bell. Bangor, County Down, N. Ireland. August 1995

Acknowledgements

First and before all, Derek and I must acknowledge how beholden we are to our respective spouses, Stefanie and Frances. Their patience and forbearance sustained us. Of my immediate family, two, our youngest sons, Eamon Tarlach and Liam Fionnbarra, missed out on due recognition in my first book, *Ólta le Ceolta*. Their summers in the Donegal Gaeltacht, in Ranafast, aroused their interest in many of the songs particularised here. Some who have been expected to encourage and help us were singularly remiss. But Dr Maurna Crozier, director of the Community Relations Council, Belfast, and her zealous coadjutors, Jean McKelvey and Pat O'Neill, with their willing typesetting team of Enterprise Technology, spurred us on and thus secured acceptance of our work. Finally, my son-in-law, Professor Michael Laver, and our Bríd, his wife, have led us to our publishers, Wolfhound.

Bail ó Dhia ortha uilig.

CHAPTER ONE

Eighteenth Century Songs

I will hold my house in the high wood,
Within a walk of the sea;
And the men that were boys when I was a boy
Shall sit and drink with me. (Hilaire Belloc)

Thanks to such renowned folk-groups as The Chieftains our Irish traditional music is lauded worldwide. Our folk-songs are not so well appreciated, on a global scale at least. Every time I listen to a fervid group of fiddlers, pleasant as their music is, I ask where are the great songs to be heard? For a half-century I have been singing these songs of the North. From 1934 to 1984, as a student and a teacher in Coláiste Bhríde (Saint Brigid's College) in the Donegal Gaeltacht I have loved the beautiful local songs.

I am a singer, not a collector. All my life I have loved the fiddle, the violin. The late Tommy Potts, believed by knowledgeable musicians to have been as influential in his time as the great Seán Ó Riada, was most gracious on the one occasion we met.

'Liam, this is Tommy Potts, the fiddler and tin-whistler.'

'What is your instrument?'

'I sing.'

'The greatest instrument of all.'

My colleague, Derek Bell, has been playing with the superb folk-musicians, The Chieftains, for over twenty years now. He is a classical musician, instrumentalist and composer. For a dozen years now we have collaborated in getting these melodies transcribed.

It is held that once a melody is written down it ceases to be traditional. Derek prefers the word *correct*. He says that if sufficient care is taken it is possible to snare the evanescent twists and twirls of our song-music. He does concede that it would necessitate writing down the music of each verse – up to dozens often enough – to follow the grace-notes and ornamentations that vary from verse to verse.

AISLING

A feature of the poets of the 'hidden Ireland' in the eighteenth century, notably in Munster, was the 'aisling'. Our first song is a South Armagh 'aisling'. Perhaps the best of them all.

The poet Art MacCooey (in South Armagh in the second half of the eighteenth century) was awakened one morning from his slumbers near the O'Neill vault in Creggan Churchyard, by Crossmaglen, by a bird's whistling. Unlike his Munster contemporaries he expected no respite from thraldom from Bonny Prince Charlie or any other dissolute Stuart. The great O'Neill family still held his allegiance; yes, even if their local stronghold, Glassdrummond Castle was overthrown.

In this aisling (vision-poem), he visualised a fairy-maiden appearing to him and trying to lure him away from his grotty existence in the cold vault, to the 'Land of Honey where Saxon had never held sway'.

When Derek Bell first heard me sing this great South Armagh song he was sure that it must have been my best. 'If it is, I have been singing it for nearly half a century.' We went over and over it, sometimes ten times for a particular verse, until he had annotated every grace-note and nuance. This version which I sing was collected by Father Luke Donnellan from Mary Harvassey, Clonalig, Crossmaglen. A lifetime later I was principal teacher in Clonalig Primary School, from 1952-60. A close friend, the late Father Frank MacFadden, curate in Upper Creggan Parish, once took me out to the eastern side of the parish to Glassdrummond. There we walked up and down Leyther Hill. The very hill where, so tradition had it, the poet had led a horse drawing manure for the landlord, Rev. Mr. Hill of Mount Hill, up and down, up and magically down a whole afternoon, the while he composed 'Úir-Chill an Chreagáin'.

[Maybe time for this note. The great Willie Clancy, prince of uillean pipers from Milltown Malbay, Co. Clare, made the startling observation, just a year or two before he died (c.1972), that he would have given all his piping to have sufficient Irish and the ability to sing one of the great slow airs well. He also infuriated many instrumentalists by laying it down that no one could play such opulent songs as 'Sal Óg Rua', 'An Clár Bog Déil', 'Na Connerys', 'Úna Bhán', 'Róisín Dubh', 'Sliabh na mBan Fionn', 'Cath Chéim an Fhia', 'Úr-Chill an Chreagáin' or 'Anach Cuain', if they had not a thorough knowledge, nuances and all, of the Irish language, so richly found in the songs.]

Úir Chill an Chreagáin

(Ure Kill an Khragg-ahin)

THE NOBLE CHURCH OF CREGGAN

1.

Ag Úir-chill a' Chreagáin sea
chodail mé aréir faoi bhrón;
Agus le h-éirí na maidne tháinig
an ainnir fá mo dhéin ie póig.
Bhí gríos-ghrua ghártha aici agus
loinnir in a cíabh mar ór;
Is gurab é íocshláinte a' domhain
bheith ag amharc ar a' ríoin óig.

By Creggan's noble vaults
I slept last night in woe;
And at early morning's dawn
I woke to a maiden's kiss.
Her ardent smiling face,
her golden gleaming hair;
And it was unutterable balm
to behold this noble queen.

2.

[The maid]
A fhiail-fhir charthanaigh ná caithtear
thusa i néalltai bróin.
Ach éirí go tapaí agus
aistrigh liom siar sa ród;
Go Tír dheas na Meala nach bhfuair
Gaill inti réim go fóill;
Is gheobhair aoibhneas ar hallai
do mo mhealladh-sa le siansa ceoil.

Gentle, loving sir, do not let
sorrow's clouds cover you;
But rise up with haste and
accompany me over the road;
To the fine Land of Honey where
Saxon never yet held sway.
And there find pleasure in our halls
and lead me astray with your strains.

3.

A ríoin deas mhilis an tú Hélen
fá'n ar tréaghadh slóight'?
Nó'n des na naoi mná deasa
Parnassus thú bhí déanta i gcló?
Cá tír ins an chruinne in ar h-oileadh thú,
a réalt gan cheo,
Le n-ar mhian leat mo shamhail-se bheith
ag cogarnaigh leat siar sa ród?

My fragrant lovely queen, are you Helen
for whom hosts were slain?
Or one of the fair beauties of
Parnassus so famous of yore?
Where in the wide world were you
nurtured, my peerless star,
That you should deign to have me
coaxing with you along the road?

On they proceed exchanging eloquent quatrains; history, classical learning in abundance. One final verse to stir Ulster hearts from then to these distracted days. The poor jobbing gardener yielding to the noble fairy-maiden.

4.

A ríoin is deise ma's cinniúin
duit mé mar stór;
Tabhair léagsa is gealladh domh ar maidin
sul má dtéim sa ród.
Ma éagaim fa'n tSeanainn, i gCríoch
Mhanainn nó fá'n Éifte mhór;
Gurab i gCill chúmhra an Chreagáin
a leagfar mé i gcré faoi fhód.

O, sweet lovely queen, if I'm fated
to win you as spouse;
Give me your solemn word this morning
before I set off on the road.
Should I die by the Shannon, by Mann or
by Egypt's great bounds;
That by Creggan's fragrant church
I be laid to my final rest.

An Sagart Ó Muirí, passionate and enterprising Gaelic scholar, thought that this other poem by Art MacCooey is even better than the acclaimed 'Úir-Chill an Chreagáin'. Another clear testimony that Ulster Gaels had no hopes of succour from dissolute Stuarts with their white cockade. Long, long after the Flight of the Earls in 1607 our Ulster poets, and pre-eminently Art Mac Cubhthaigh, looked to the scions of the great O'Neill for deliverance. Their bastion in south-east Armagh, Glassdrummond Castle, might be gone and the storied rooks with it. Eoghan Rua, long after the Battle of the Yellow Ford, was still a name of pride.

The great, widespreading Dunreavy Wood is the poet's theme. Reputed to stretch twenty miles or more, 'Ye cud ha' swung the miles and miles from here to Newry, without having to touch ground. Mighty oaks that took 300 years to mature, cut down and sold off at sixpence a-piece to make their mighty "ships of the line".'

Aige Bruach Dhún Réimhe

(Egga Broo-ach Ghoon Rave-eh)

DUNREAVY WOOD

The poet, now a poor farm-labourer, peals out in sonorous verse matched by a fitting melody, this lament and eulogy.

1.

Aige bruach Dhún Réimhe ar uaigneas lae,
ba shnuamhar géaga bláth geal.
Chualas géimneach cuantaí Eireann agus
fuaim sa spéir in airde.
Na dúile i bpian is a gcúl le chéile's
gnúis na gréine báite;
Is slua na n-éan ag fuagradh scéil
le cumha gur éag na cága.

By Dunreavy Wood on a lonesome day
the bright blooming trees were splendid.
I heard Ireland's booming seas and
the skies on high were throbbing.
All nature in pain, all in disarray;
and drowned the face of the sun.
And the host of birds proclaimed the tale
that the castle rooks were gone.

2.

Tráth thiontaigh 'n spéir is gach ní faoi 'n ghréin,
is an saol faoi éiclips áiféal';
Smaoineas féin gur mithid dom téicheadh go
Dún na gcraobh is na fáilte.
D'éirigh a' smolach cúmhra béilbhinn suas ar
ghéagán lámh liom.
Is ba bhinne na téadaí milse Orphéus ceiliúr
an éin is áilne.

Once the sky overturned and all 'neath the sun,
all life in a fabled eclipse,
I thought to myself that it behooved me to go
to Dundalk of the woods and welcomes.
The fragrant, sweet-voiced thrush soared high,
up on this branch beside me.
And Orpheus's lute, with its sweet-tuned strings,
never matched this bird so lovely.

3.

A smólaí chléibh, ó tchí tú féin gur claoiodh
sliocht Ghael san áit seo;
Tabhair iarraidh 'e léim i lúbaí an aeir, is beir
siodamh i gcéin thar sáile.
Mar a bhfuíghfear fréimh de ghaoil Uí Néill
i dtíortha tréana Spainne;
Agus aithris don fhréimh sin a mhaireas gan éag gur
scaoileadh a n-aol-chloich áluinn.

O darling thrush, since you clearly see the Gael
laid low in this place;
Take a leap on high in the whorls of the air, and bear
solace abroad over the ocean.
Where you'll find the scions of Ó Néill's clan
in mighty Spanish dominions;
And recall to those scions that still survive that
their lime-white walls are shattered.

4.

Eoghan Rua, mo léan thú bheith fuar i gcré;
Is tú a ruaigfeadh na ceithearnaigh Ghallda;
Agus fuadaíodh Féilim uasal tréitheach
Suas go Laighean d'a bhás a fháil.
Tiarna Uibh Éathach bhí ar uaislibh Gaeil,
Gur chríonnaigh an t-éag a chnámha.
Is cá bhfuighfear a léithéid arís chun féidhme,
Ó síneadh an méid seo i gclárthaí?

Owen Roe, alas you're cold in the clay;
You'd have routed the Saxon churls.
And noble gifted Phelim snatched away
To Leinster to die there.
Lord Iveagh the noblest of Gaels,
Till death laid his bones to rot.
And where now will any come to direct our lives,
Since such as these were buried?

CHAPTER TWO

Modern Love-Songs

Séamus Ó Gríanna (James Greene) is in direct succession to the O'Donnell brothers, all seven of them poets. Later we tell more of the O'Donnells. They flourished, nearly two centuries ago in Ranafast, in the beautiful if desolate Gaeltacht area of western Donegal. Our contemporary scions of their line, Séamus and his brother Seosamh, are acknowledged prose stylists in modern Gaelic literature. A third brother Seán was the most poetic. But Séamus had a knacky gift of writing fine lyrics to lovely melodies. Just as the *nonpareil* Robert Burns did with the old Scots airs for his 'bonnie' lyrics.

The lyricist, Séamus Ó Gríanna, surely the last one we'd have visualised in the 1930s as a soft swain; but he was, in love with a beautiful lady, apparently much too old for him. In the South of France seeking some respite for his poor health.

He was a prolific writer in Gaelic prose, novels and short stories; remarkable mostly for their easy, felicitous style. He used his grandmother's name, Máire, as his *nom de plume.* He certainly had her storytelling gift of the *seanchaí.* Some pundits hold that the Irish with the Arabs and the people of India are the world's best storytellers. Non-pundits held that Séamus Ó Gríanna had no music in him. He may not have been a singer but few modern Gaelic lyricists can match his songs.

Tráthnóna Beag Aréir

(Trah-noh-nah Behg Ah-rair)

It is not easy to Anglicise this title, perhaps because it is so quintessentially a Gaeltacht song. Literally, 'Little Evening Last Night'. Temptation to call it that. But the summer evening is sinking to rest, dew falling. So, 'Late Last Evening'.

1.

Thíos i lár a ghleanna,
tráthnóna beag aréir;
Agus driúcht na ndeora geala
'na luí ar bharr an fhéir.
Sea casadh dom-sa 'n ainnir
a b'áilne gnúis is pearsa;
Sí sheol mo stuaim 'un seachráin,
tráthona beag aréir.

Curfá

Agus a Rí nár lách ár n-ealaíon,
gabháil síos an gleann aréir;
Ag éalodh fríd a chanach
agus ciúineas ins a spéir.
Ó, a rún mo chléibh nár mhilis
ár súgradh croí 's nár ghoirid?
Is a Rí na glóire gile,
tabhair aráis an oích' aréir.

2.

Do chiabh-fholt fáinneach frasach,
do mhalaidh bhán, do dhéad;
Do chaol-choim áluinn maiseach agus
glórthaí caoine do bhéil.
Do bhrá mar chluimh na h-eala,
do shúil mar réalt na maidne.
Agus fairíor gur dhual dúinn scaradh,
tráthnóna beag aréir.

Curfá

1.

Down in the heart of the valley,
as evening waned last night.
As the dewdrops faintly glistened,
lying heavy on the grass.
'Twas then I met this maiden,
so lovely and so winsome;
She drove my wits astray,
as evening waned last night.

Chorus

And dear Lord, how serene our meeting,
as we strolled down the glen.
Gliding through bog-cotton
while silence filled the sky.
And oh! my love, how sweet it was,
our courting, and how brief.
And King of eternal glory,
please give us back last night.

Your fine locks, crowned with ringlets;
your fair brow and your teeth.
Your shapely lovely waist and
the sweet sounds from your lips.
Your bosom like a swan's down;
your eye the morning star;
And alas! we had to sever,
as the evening waned last night.

Chorus

Reliable testimony has it that she was really a beautiful woman. She died not long after. But what encomiums of her beauty! Note too how although Yeats still found old people in Mayo who remembered Mary Hynes' beauty two lifetimes after; her memory is green now a century later still because Raftery, the great Western poet (1779 - 1835), sang:

'Sí Máire Ní Eidhín an stáid-bhean bhéasach.'

(Mary Hynes is a stately beauty.)

So with Máire's great love. Now, in spite of Church interdiction of 'all superstitions, charms and spells', we get the usual Gaelic hyperbole.

3.

Dá bhfaghainn-se 'rís cead pilleadh
agus labhairt le stór mo chléibh
Nó dá bhfhaghainn-se bua ar chinniún
chár mhiste liom fá'n tsaol.
Shiúlfainn leat fríd chanach,
fríd mhéilte 'r chíumhas na mara;
Agus dúiche Dé dá gcaillfinn
go bpógfainn-se do bhéal.

Curfá

If I got leave to return and
speak to my true love.
Or if I could conquer fate
life would not mean so much.
We'd wend through bog-cotton,
through the sand-dunes by the shore;
And even should I lose God's heaven
I still would kiss your mouth.

Chorus

Ba Loinnireach Grian an Tráthnóna

(Bah Linn-yirr-ach Grain an Tráh-noh-nah)

BRIGHT SHINING EVENING

Some might fault the author for choosing a Moore's melody for his lyrics. With all respect, any singer worth a damn must revel in the sheer artistry of the lyrics in the *Melodies*. Bunting was furious that 'his' tunes had been stolen by Moore; after all the laborious noting-down of the great melodies at the Belfast Harp Festival of 1792.

Moore had earned a fortune from the fruits of Bunting's toil. But as Derek Bell has shown elsewhere Bunting took certain liberties with the melodies he took down.

For me, when Ó Grianna chose this melody, 'Has Sorrow Thy Young Days Shaded?', for his lyrics he clinched the argument.

This Moore Melody, chosen by Séamus Ó Grianna for his lovely verses, is in Derek's words: 'Pentatonic flavour, very characteristic of many of Moore's melodies.'

1.

Ba loinnnireach grian a' tráthnóna
is ba bhinn guth an éin ar chraoibh;
Nuair a casadh liom ainnir na n-órfholt,
is mé a' siúl chois trá liom féin.
Nach gasta chuaidh dealramh na gréine
i bhfolach faoi néaltai ceo;
Ó's nár ghoirid ár súgradh le chéile,
gur éalaigh tú uaim go deo.

How brilliant the sunshine that evening;
how sweet sounded the bird on the bough.
When I met the golden-haired lady,
as I strolled all alone on the strand.
How fleeting the gleam of the sun there;
hidden beneath misty clouds.
And how brief was our trysting together,
till you slipped away from me, for good.

For years I was uneasy with the second verse where the lovesick boy is in no way loth to tell how bitterly he wept for his departed love. Shakespeare's oft-quoted 'Men have died and worms have eaten them,/But not for love' seemed more resolute. Years, however, put manners and understanding on us all. Tears are shed. Why ever not?

2.

Is tuirseach is brónach mo shaol-sa,
is mé ag imeacht liom féin faoi smúid.
Is corrach mo chodladh san oíche,
's ni bheidh mise beo gan tú.
A chéadsearc a' gcluin tú mé 'g caoineadh,
nó nach trua leat fein mo lui ?
Gan aonduine le theacht ar mo ghaobhair,
a thógfadh a' cian seo díom ?

How wearisome and woeful my life now,
as I wander about so depressed.
How unsettled each night's sleeping;
I can't live without yourself.
My darling, do you not hear my weeping?
Has your pity no place where I lie?
I have no one around here to visit;
to try and allay my plight.

3.

Is mairg gur casadh dom riamh thú,
'spéirbhean na gcuachann fionn.
Is go bhfuilthear a' mo chlaoí is a' mo chríathrú,
's mé a' meabhrú 'r ghlór do chinn.
Ní chluinfidh mé guth binn a' smaolaigh
a' seinm ar ghéag níos mó.
Ó's nár ghoirid ár súgradh le chéile
gur éalaigh tú uaim go deo.

Too bad that I ever met you,
my true love, fair-ringletted queen.
And I still sorely tormented to recall
the soft tones of your voice.
No more will I hear now the song-thrush
as it sings so free on the bough.
And how brief was our courting together
till you slipped away from me for good.

Is Cianach Corrach

(Iss Kane-ach Kurrach)

Bothered, Unsettled

Reiteration again here that all we do and can do is give the melodies as faithfully learnt and transcribed; give the lyrics as correctly as possible. Then hope that some savour of it all can be gained. Our lyricist, Jimmy Ellimy (as Séamus was known locally), chose a beautiful melody associated in the South of Ireland with a fine love-song, 'Jimmy Mo Mhíle Stór', for this lament for his lost love. The second verse is particularly felicitous. A genuine *frisson* each time it is sung.

1.

Is cianach corrach a chodail
mé 'n oiche 'réir;
Is ba bhrónach m'aigneadh ar
maidin le spéarthaí 'n lae.
Tá ualach tinnis 'gus tuirse
ar lár mo chléibh...
Is, a Rí na cruinne, nach
dona mar fágadh mé.

Bothered, unsettled I went
to sleep last night.
And with the clouds of dawn
my mind was still oppressed.
I'm burdened, I'm weary, I'm ill
in the depth of my breast;
And, Lord Almighty, how
desolate here I'm left.

2.

D'éirigh an ghealach 'gus
chealg sí an saol 'un suain;
Agus spréidh sí a solus mar
fhallaing ar mhéilte 'n chuain.
Crónán an easa gur dheise
'ná glórthaí píob,
Agus tuaim na tuinne
gur bhinne 'na ceoltaí sí.

Up rose the moon to soothe
the world asleep;
Spreading her beams as a mantle
on the dunes by the sea.
This murmurous waterfall more
tuneful than the piper's play,
And the swish of the waves even
sweeter than fairy strains.

3.

Ó, 'a mhaighdean mhaiseach, tar seal
a' mo chomhair ar chuairt;
Is cóirigh mo leaba le sgrátha 's le
fóide fuar';
Cealg mé a chodladh le
glórthaí do bhéilín bhinn,
I n-uaigneas a' ghleann'
'inar casadh le chéile sinn.

O, my lovely sweetheart, please
come to me, visit me now,
And lay out my poor bed with
scraws and damp cold sods.
Coax me to sleep with your
songs in your tuneful voice;
In that lonely glen, that
glen where we first met.

CHAPTER THREE

Glens of Antrim Songs

Many a night's crack in the Glens of Antrim my wife and I had with two Cushendun men, Eddie Brogan and Pat MacCormack. The latter was proud to be living in the same townland as did Seán MacAmbrois (John MacCambridge). In the bad years of the last century Seán had determined to leave his lovely glen. He could make no go of it, either farming or fishing. But how to leave all behind? Still, in the country expression, 'he be to go'. Go he must. The final night was a glory. The full moon shining serenely on the Sea of Moyle murmuring below; the Dun river rippling by; Glen Dun stretched before him; the high rise of the Antrim plateau a background.

Seán MacAmbrois was so overcome by the prospect of exile that he composed this heartbreaking song. It is disputed whether he was to go into exile in Scotland. But there was only a short enough boat-trip across, that was often enough rowed. Or was he to go into exile to North America? That passage has been rowed in our day by the English soldier, Shay Bligh. Whether or which, Seán's song so overcame him that he changed his mind; stayed at home. Prospered.

Visualizing himself in exile, he was constrained to compose:

Airdí Cuain

(Aarjee Kooahn)

The Heights of Cushendun

1.

Dá mbéinn féin i nAirdí Cuain;
In aice an tsléibh' úd tá i bhfad uaim;
B'annamh liom gan tul ar chuairt
Go Gleann na gCuach Dia Domhnaigh.

If I were back in Cushendun near
that peak so distant now;
I'd rarely enough miss making a trip to
Glen Dun on a Sunday.

Loinneog

Agus och! och! Éire uilig is ó!
Éire lionndubh agus ó!
Sé mo chroí tá trom is brónach.

Refrain

And, oh! alas for Ireland and all!
Ireland, black depression and all!
I'm heartsore and sorrowful.

2.

'Siomaí Nollaig is mé liom féin;
I mBun Abhann Doinne is mé gan chéill;
Ag iomáin ar a' Trá Bhán,
Mo chamán bán 'mo dhorn liom.

Many's a Christmas Day alone,
carefree enough in Cushendun;
I'd be hurling on the White Strand,
gripping my white camán.

Loinneog

Refrain

3.

Nach tursach mise anseo liom féin?
Nach n-aithnim guth coiligh,
londubh nó traon?
Gealbhán, smaolach, naoscach féin
Is chá n-aithnim féin an Domhnach?

How weary now I find myself.
No woodcock, blackbird
or corncrake here,
Sparrow, missel-thrush, even a snipe.
Sure I don't know when it's Sunday.

Loinneog

Refrain

4.

Dá mbeadh agam féin coite 's rámha,
Nó go n-iomarainn leis a' tsnámh;
Dúil as Dia go sroichfinn slán,
Is go bhfaghainn-se bás in Éirinn.

If I only had a skiff and oars,
That I might row with the tide;
Trust in God to arrive safe;
And to find death in Ireland.

Loinneog

Refrain

Sponsored by Irish and Scottish Arts Councils, small groups of poets and musicians alternately visit their fellow Celts. In 1977 I was a singer in such a group, flying in an eight-seater plane of Logan Air; from Edinburgh to bare treeless Tiree, landing on a little airstrip. Next day, down on the beach, this time at low tide, at Barra. The following day's destination, Stornaway. The fourth day by a little steamer, a blazing sunny sky; were we in the isles of Greece? Landed at Port Ree on Skye. The greatest living Celtic poet, Somhairle MacLean, there to greet us with friendly warmth. Every evening on each Hebridean island we sang and played and poetised. All our hosts, mainly fervid Free Presbyterians (Barra's priest, Father MacNeill, of our faith), vied as Gaidhling speakers in taking the Gaelic guests of Ireland to their hearts. Everywhere they joined lustily in singing from the hall in accord with the soloists, as warmly as Welsh rugby folk in Cardiff Arms Park. Lucky for me that my native County Antrim, at Ballycastle – well, really at Rathlin Island, just off the coast there, the same Rathlin with the legendary tale of Robert the Bruce and the Spider – had provided me with 'The Boatman', 'Fear an Bháta'. Rathlin's Gaelic was as much Gaidhling as theirs once. The song was my unfailing bait. They loved it.

Fear an Bháta = Fear an Bháid

(Fahr ah Wahta)

THE BOATMAN

Verse 1

circa ♩. = 60

Loinneog

'fhir a' bháta, is ná hó-ró éile,
'fhir a' bháta, is ná hó-ró éile,
'fhir a' bháta, is ná hó-ró éile,
Mo shoraidh slán leat gach áit an dtéid thú.

Refrain

Boatman, my boatman, ho-ro for ever.
Boatman, my boatman, ho-ro for ever.
Boatman, my boatman, ho-ro for ever.
Goodbye to all each place you go.

1.

Théid me suas ar an chnoc is airde;
Féach an bhfeic mé fear an bháta.
An dtig tú anocht nó an dtig tu amárach?
Nó muna dtig thú idir is trua atá mé.

I go up on the hill; to see if I'd see
my bonny boatman.
Will you come tonight or come tomorrow?
Or if you don't come how pitiful I am.

Loinneog

Refrain

2.

Tá mo chroí-se briste brúite
Is tric na ndeor a rith bhó mo shúilean.
An dtig tú inniu nó am bidh mé 'súil leat?
Nó an druid mé an doras le h-osna thúirseach?

My heart is sorely troubled.
The track of my tears is from my eyes.
Will you come today or shall I await you?
Or shall I close the door with a weary sigh?

Loinneog

Refrain

3.

Thug mé gaol duit is chan fhéad mé áthrú;
Chá gaol bliana is chá gaol ráithe.
Ach gaol ó thoiseacht, nuair bha mé 'mo pháiste;
Is nach seasc a choíche mé 'gur chloígh an bás mé?

I pledged my troth that I can never alter,
Not for a year nor a quarter's length.
But pledged from my childhood's years;
Won't I be worthless till death conquers all?

Loinneog

Refrain

SANDHILLS OF KHANDOORAN

Derek says of this melody: 'beautiful and lyrical. Probably too well-known to go into the book, yet also too beautiful to leave out.' So too, the lyricist, Séamus Ó Gríanna, with fine taste wed his lyrics on his native Khandooran to this Antrim melody.

The blue hills of Antrim I see in my dreams;
The high hills of Antrim, her glens and her streams.
In sunlight or in shadow, in weal or in woe,
The sweet vision haunts me, wherever I go.

This time let us go right on to the fine lyrics of Séamus Ó Gríanna. The author was noted perhaps more for the felicity of his style than for his gifts as a novelist. He has left some splendid songs. Here again he has left a superb song, particularly in the third verse.

Méilte Cheann Dubhrann

(Mell-cheh Khann-doorann)

SANDHILLS OF KHANDOORAN

1.

A Mhéilte Cheann Dubhrann sibh
a thógfadh dom cian;
Tráthnona sa tsámhradh
nuair a luíos a' ghrian.
Nach aoibhinn do do chladaigh
d'oíche 's de ló;
Is a Mhéilte Cheann Dubhrann
céad slán libh go deo.

Sandhills of Khandooran
you'd cure all my cares;
On fine summer eves as
the sun sinks to rest.
How pleasant your strands
by night and by day;
Oh, sandhills of Khandooran,
my last sad farewell.

These lines may seem banal, even maudlin, to the stranger, but step down to the reaches of that western ocean. Walk those rolling strands. Watch a flurry of oyster-catchers. Scarely a tree for miles; even the bushes are stunted, blown back from the prevailing western winds. Larks spin in their harmonious spirals high and higher. Then sing the song.

2.

Nach sna Méilte udaigh 'chaith mé
seal aoibhinn gan ghruaim;
A' buachailleacht eallaigh
fá imeall a' chuain?
Is ann a bogadh mo chliabhán
nuair a bhí mé beag óg.
Is a Mhéilte Cheann Dubhrann,
céad slán libh go deo.

In those same sandhills
how carefree I played,
Or minded the cows by
the edge of the bay.
There my cradle was rocked,
when I was a babe;
And sandhills of Khandooran,
my last sad farewell.

3.

Tá néaltai na maidne
a' breacadh sa spéir;
Tá na coiligh a' scairtigh
le bánu 'n lae.
Tá 'n soitheach a' fanacht
in imeall a' cheo;
Is a Mhéilte Cheann Dubhrann
céad slán libh go deo.

The clouds of the morning
are speckling the sky;
The cockerels are crowing
as the dawn comes awake.
The vessel lies waiting on
the fringe of the fog;
And sandhills of Khandooran,
my last sad farewell.

CHAPTER FOUR

From Lough Neagh to Slieve Gallen

Ballindrum and Mowillian were well represented,
The Loup, Ballyneill and Doliskey were there.
From Tulnagee down to sweet Ballygrooby
Were all doing business in Blackberry Fair.

Until 1945 when I married, my mind was set on the Gaelic songs alone. The Gaelic songs are incomparable. But when I first came to live in the country, in County Derry, teaching in Counties Tyrone, Armagh, Antrim and Donegal I discovered local 'bards' had emulated, perhaps unconsciously, their Gaelic forebears.

Verses and songs like these country ballads alerted me to other fine songs besides my songs in Irish. The parish priest of the Loup assured me that my father-in-law, John Corey, the Bard of Moneymore, was 'the best-read man on a few books he had ever known'. Signs of it when we come to the potted history in the fourth verse.

THE ROSE OF MONEYMORE

This song was written to accommodate a neighbouring lad going off to America. He wanted some verses to laud his sweetheart and his home place.

Apropos verse 4, our first little daughter, Fionnuala, then only three and a half years old, was with us one day as we passed Conyngham's Spring Hill, Moneymore. 'There are the trees that your grandfather, John Corey, wrote about in his song.'

'Which one is the Tree of Liberty?'

The Rose of Moneymore

1.

Farewell to dear old Ireland,
I can no longer stay;
I now shake hands and bid farewell,
I'm for Amerikay.
Our good ship lies in deep Lough Foyle,
it's bound for New York's shore;
Which bids me say, 'Farewell, Ardtrea,
and you, sweet Moneymore.'

2.

I was born in Country Derry, boys,
I'm not ashamed to tell,
Near that sweet spot they call the Loup,
I'm sure you know it well.
And there a charming maid resides,
and often I have sworn
To make her mine when I return
to you, sweet Moneymore.

3.

This little town encircled round
with many a woodland grove,
Where lads and lasses they do meet
in pleasure for to rove.
Its verdant hills and shamrock braes
that oft I wandered o'er;
And by my side the girl I loved,
the Rose of Moneymore.

4.

George Washington Columbia freed
from the British Lion's claws;
And on it planted Freedom's Tree,
from out which sprang good laws.
Come on my boys, be of good cheer,
we'll try again once more;
To plant the Tree of Liberty
on the braes of Moneymore.

5.

Our Irishmen have been run down
for centuries gone by,
Because they loved their motherland
and ne'er would it deny.
Our fathers fought and died for it
round Ireland's lovely shores,
And beat the Saxon ten to one
on the braes of Moneymore.

6.

Then farewell to dear old Ireland,
I can no longer stay.
Our good ship sails tomorrow,
it's time we were away.
So fill your glasses to the brim
and toast with one loud roar,
The verdant hills and shamrock braes
and the Rose of Moneymore.

BLACKBERRY FAIR

The tune here is from a rollicking Cork ballad eulogising a 'heroic' champion hurler, 'The Boul' Thady Quill'. The lyrics concern a fair organised a full hundred years ago by the local 'big house'; the local country folk were gathering blackberries to sell at presumably low rates. The 'Bard' was irked by their exploitation.

Some forty years ago an 'old residenter' assured me that 'Johnny's song killed the Fair'. Good as the name of the Conynghams has been in this century, they went amiss, apparently, then. The Bard of Moneymore was too honest, too fair-minded, to attack such a Fair if it were even half-straightforward. More power to the Bard.

Derek arís: 'Derivative of other tunes. But very fine in itself.'

Blackberry Fair

1.

Ye muses of note, I pray you'll assist me,
And help me this line or two for to write down.
For I am bereaved and my heart sorely grieved,
For the blackberry maidens of Moneymore town.
I chanced in September to take a short ramble
Around by sweet Springhill to banish dull care;
When I met twenty lasses with carts and jackasses
All marching in rows to the Blackberry Fair.

Chorus

Ye briary lads and briary lasses,
I'll do my endeavours your feelings to spare;
But farming and weaving have gone to the devil,
Since the Conynghams started their Blackberry Fair.

2.

I must sympathise with these daughters of Éireann;
Their equal I never have met with before.
It pains me to see them in such a condition,
All selling their soft goods in old Moneymore.
Their hands and their faces are daubed and besmeared,
On every inch is a cut or a tear.
Their friends or their sweethearts
  would scarce recognise them,
If they e'er chanced to meet them in Blackberry Fair.

Chorus

3.

I kindly enquired of one of these fair ones,
How far she had come on that bright shining day.
She told me she'd come there from far Ballinderry,
And pointed out several that came from Lough Fea.
Ballindrum and Mowillian were well represented;
The Loup, Ballyneill and Doluskey were there.
From Tulnagee down to sweet Ballygrooby
Were all doing business in Blackberry Fair.

Chorus

4.

I thought I would wander up to the market,
To see how the business was going that day.
There were some had come down from the
  face of Slieve Gallen,
While others came up from the shores of Lough Neagh.
Some people were praising the Conynghams highly,
While others were trying their books for to square.
To their Ladyships 'credit' they'd give no longer;
It was 'cash' that they wanted in Blackberry Fair.

Chorus

5.

I now give advice to these lads and lasses:
They all have been duped in this briary trade.
Till now and forever give over ditch-breaking,
And take to the weaving, the shovel and spade.
Leave such dirty work to the landlords and agents,
Bailiffs, policemen and such other ware.
And never again let me see your sweet faces,
In any damned spot like their Blackberry Fair.

Chorus

SLIABH GALLEN'S BRAE

This, possibly our best Northern ballad, appears worthily enough here; it was made by John Corey's cousin; maybe only second or third cousin; we don't know for sure. Like Raftery in 'Mary Hynes' or 'Rantin' roamin' Robbie' Burns, the poet proudly asserts authorship in the verse. A telling point has been made that part of the piquancy of this song comes from the repetition of the word 'bonny' in each final line, much as in that mysterious poem by Robert Frost where the magical note is sounded with repetition:

The woods are lovely, dark, and deep,
But I have promises to keep,
And miles to go before I sleep;
And miles to go before I sleep.

1.

As I went a-walking one morning in May,
To view yonder valleys and mountains so gay,
I was thinking of yon flowers
soon a-going to decay,
That grow around you bonny, bonny
Sliabh Gallen's Brae.

2.

My name is James MacGarvey and
I'd have you understand,
I come from Derrygennard and I own a farm of land.
But my rents are getting higher and I can no longer pay.
So farewell unto you bonny, bonny
Sliabh Gallen's Brae.

3.

Oft o'er those mountains with my dog and my gun,
I wandered those mountains for pastime and fun.
But those days are now all over
and I must go away.
So farewell unto you bonny, bonny
Sliabh Gallen's Brae.

4.

It's not for the want of employment at home,
That causes the sons of Old Ireland to roam.
But our rents are getting higher and
the rates we cannot pay.
So farewell unto you bonny, bonny
Sliabh Gallen's Brae.

5.

Farewell to Old Ireland, that island so green,
To the parish of Lissan and
the Cross of Ballinascreen.
May good fortune shine on you while I am far away.
So farewell unto you bonny, bonny
Sliabh Gallen's Brae.

THE OLD CROSS OF ARDBOE

Through a teacher friend in Tyrone, I got a letter from a butcher in Coalisland. So I came in contact with the work of the 'Poet' Canavan, 'Nelly's John' from Killycolpy, near Stewartstown. He died in 1921. He was unable to write his verses. His sister did so on unused pieces of wallpaper. These were stored in the 'farry', a hole in the jamb-wall, by the chimney. Times when the chimney went a-fire, the paper burned, the verses were lost. 'Old Ardboe' has stuck in my mind for nearly a half-century.

The Old Cross of Ardboe

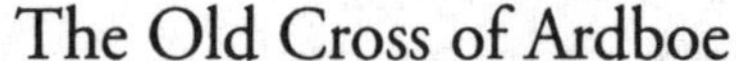

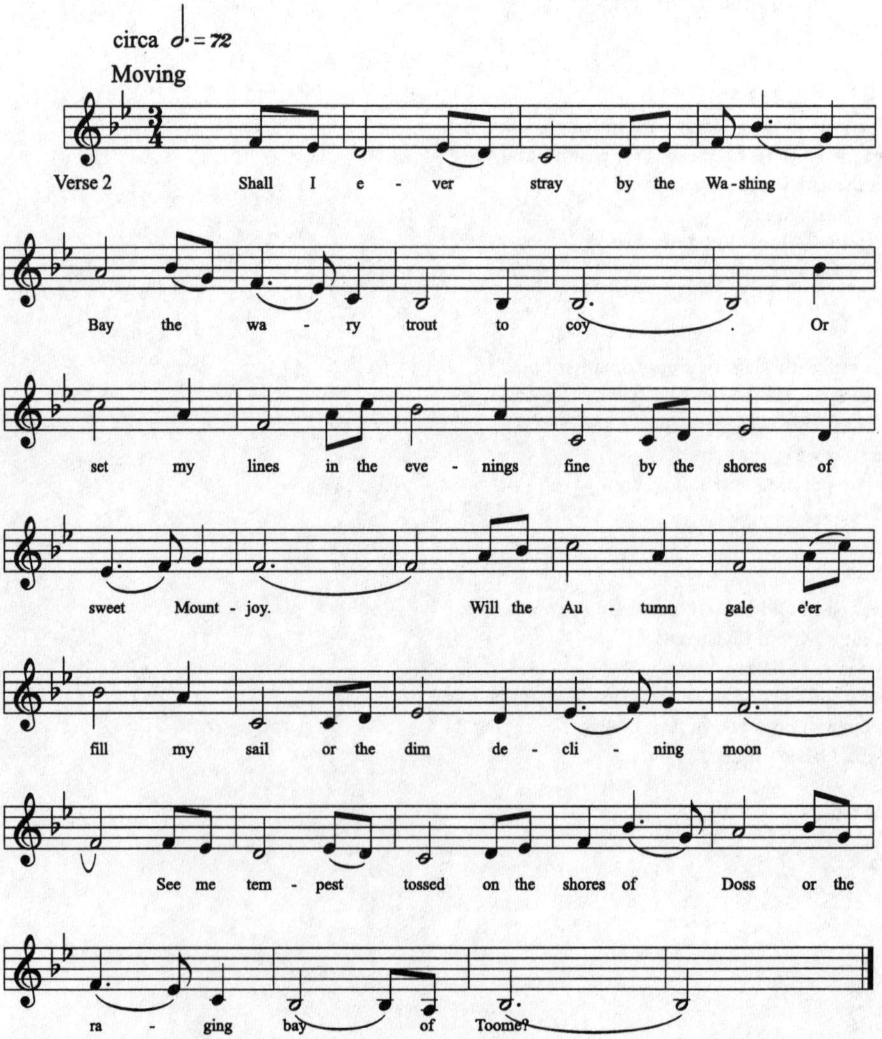
circa = 72
Moving
Verse 2 Shall I e - ver stray by the Wa - shing
Bay the wa - ry trout to coy. Or
set my lines in the eve - nings fine by the shores of
sweet Mount - joy. Will the Au - tumn gale e'er
fill my sail or the dim de - cli - ning moon
See me tem - pest tossed on the shores of Doss or the
ra - ging bay of Toome?

1.

Farewell, ye lovely tree-clad hills,
Farewell, ye shamrocks green.
Ye verdant banks of deep Lough Neagh,
With your silvery, winding streams.
Though far from home in green Tyrone,
Ay, far from you I've strayed;
I adore you, Killycolpy,
Where I spent my childhood days.

2.

Shall I ever stray by the Washing Bay,
The wary trout to coy,
Or set my lines in the evenings fine,
By the shores of deep Mountjoy?
Will the autumn gale e'er fill my sail,
Or the dim, declining moon
See me tempest-tossed on the shores of Doss,
Or the raging Bay of Toome?

3.

Shall I ever rove by Belmont's Grove,
Or Carnan's lofty hill;
Or hear again the fairy tales
Of the rath behind the Mill?
Shall my eyes behold Shane's Castle bold,
Or gaze on Massereene?
Will my cot e'er land on the banks of Bann,
Coney Island or Roskeen?

4.

And though, alas, long years have passed,
Still I toast that beauteous isle.
And short or long on that land of song
May the star of Freedom smile.
May plenty bloom from the Bann to Toome,
And the shamrocks verdant grow
Green round those graves near Lough Neagh's waves,
And the Old Cross of Ardboe.

CHAPTER FIVE

The Poet Mac Gríanna

Just as the seven O'Donnell brothers, poets all, flourished nearly two centuries ago in Rann na Feirste, County Donegal, so did three of their direct descendants in our day. Seosamh Mac Gríanna (Joseph Greene), the master of prose, whose percipient book of literary criticism on Pádraig Ó Conaire, another noted writer, and other themes will still, I feel sure, be read avidly in 2095; Séamus, master of prose and verse – we sampled his well-wrought wares in our Chapter Two; and Seán Bán, the youngest. He stayed at home, an albino, his eyesight very weak; his education was limited to the national school; but he enjoyed the status of *ollamh* (professor), in what Cardinal Tomás Ó Fiaich – a noted Gaelic scholar himself – called the university of the Gaeltacht, St Brigid's College, Rann na Feirste. Seán was a repository of a rich oral tradition of song and poetry and folklore equally with his two brothers; but his own songs are his golden crown.

Our song here is his impassioned retort to the lady teacher from County Antrim who spurned him a whole lifetime ago. What a beginning to a love-song: 'Here's my curse on all women.' He could even say, 'Well, hell roast all women.'

This is one of the very first of Seán Bán's lyrics that caught my fancy, back in the 1930s.

Seo Mo Mhallacht

(Shaw Muh Wallacht)

Here's My Curse on Women

1.

Seo mo mhallacht ar na mná,
Siad a mhearaigh mé is rinne mo chrá.
Thuit mé i dtús mo shaoil i ngrá,
Le spéarbhean áluinn óg.
Ó! mheall sí le na glórthaí mé.

Damn all women is my cry;
They've destroyed me, left me smashed.
In my early youth I fell in love,
With a beauty, young and fair.
Oh! her talk led my heart astray.

2.

Sí bhí sochmaí lách gan bhród;
Sí ba mheallachaí is ba mhilse póg.
Sí bhi caoithiúil ceanúil cóir;
Is ní bréag a bhfuil mé á rá;
Gur mheall sí le na glórthaí mé.

Gentle, soft and modest too;
So alluring, sweet to kiss.
Kindly, loving, all things nice;
It was never a lie to say
That her talk led my heart astray.

3.

Anois tá mé breoite caite críon,
Gan tlacht gan rath gan stór gan mhaoin;
Gan aon duine le theacht a' mo chomhair san oích'.
A thógfadh díomsa cian.
Ó! mheall sí le n-a glórthaí mé.

Now, sick, worn-out, all spent,
Listless, luckless, fortune lost.
With never a one to call at night,
To raise my drooping mind.
Oh! her talk led my heart astray.

4.

Ach dá bhfaghainn-se an saol seo ar mo mhian;
Scéal cinnte go mbeadhmuis óg a choích'.
Ná chuirfinn-se lámh na cloige arís
Go dtí an t-am ar bhfiú bheith beo;
Nuair a mheall sí le n-a glórthaí mé.

But if I could have my life as I wished,
One sure thing: we'd be ever young.
For I'd surely turn back the clock,
To when we were truly alive;
When her talk led my heart astray.

From my first days in Rann na Feirste in 1934 I was enamoured of Seán Bán. He sang quite melodiously, played the fiddle, sometimes discordantly; but always, over a period of two score years, he was making splendid songs. It was my privilege to sing them. He generously averred, 'Achan bhliain a thig tú aráis músclannn tú meisce na h-éigse ionnam.' (Every year on your return you arouse the poetic frenzy in me.) With his songs, with Hughie Devanney's singing, and with Derek Bell's musicking my cup has flowed over and over, singularly enriching me. Just as such great fiddlers as John Simey Doherty and Neilly Boyle were quick to acknowledge the authority of the master-fiddler from Scotland, Scott Skinner, so too were our folk-songs influenced across the narrow if treacherous seas. Our melody is a very familiar one.

Mo Mhúirnín Óg

(Mo Whoor-neen Awg)

My Young Darling

1.

Glaoím ort, a mhúirnín óg;
Glaoím ort, a mhíle stór.
Tar agus labhair liom uair nó dhó,
Go n-insidh mé mo scéal duit.

Hear my call, my own young love;
Hear me call, my dearest pet.
Come and chat a while or two,
Till I tell my tale of love to you.

Loinneog

Is a mhúirnín óg a mhíle ghrá.
A mhúirnín óg is tú rinne mo chrá.
Is a mhúirnin óg nach fada an lá,
Ó gheall tú mise phósadh?

Refrain

And my own young love, my dearest pet;
My own young love, my own torment.
My darling one, how long the day
Since you first said you'd wed me.

2.

Seal a bím a' déanamh bróin;
Seal beag eile' déanamh ceoil;
Seal a' meabhrú ar mo dhóigh,
Is a' gol fá'n mhnaoí nach bhfuair mé.

Whiles I feel disconsolate;
Whiles again I sit and sing.
Whiles I still recall my woes
And weep for the lass I didn't win.

Loinneog

Refrain

3.

Nuair a théim go tigh an óil,
Agus shuím síos le gloine 'r bórd.
Báithim dhá dtrian bróin sa bheoir,
Agus scilim rún mo chroí 'mach.

When to the alehouse I make my way,
And I sit me down with my glass on the board,
I drown two-thirds of my woe in the beer,
And release my deepest woes there.

Loinneog

Refrain

THE RAKISH WENCHER

This madcap song wedded to a lively double-jig, 'The Wee Duck', gives us Seán Bán at his best. In lines five and six of the first verse he flies off in a plethora of liquid 'l's. You can have your 'mellow ousel fluting in the elms'; or the hackneyed 'lake water lapping with low sound by the shore'; but no clotted blackberries of Seamus Heaney are richer than Seán Bán's *tour de force*. He tells of all the fair ones, so enamoured of him. But his health suffered for all the philandering. Finally he expressed repentance. Even then, however, he swung round in a defiant finale. Rabelais or Robbie Burns could scarcely outdo our Irish Casanova who kissed and told and to hell with the consequences.

An Banaí Drabhlasach

(Ann Bah-nee Drow-lass-ach)

The Rakish Wencher

1.

Nuair a bhí mise óg ó ba deas is ba dóighiúil,
A' scafaire stócaigh mé i súl na mban óg;
Bhínn a mealladh 's a bpógadh,
is shiúlainn a' ród leo;
Is bhínn carthanach cóir leo
gan mhairg is brón.
Bhíodh rosca gach bruinneal
a' lasadh le loinnir;
Is gach dealramh níos glaine le lúcháire romham;
Is mo ghuth-sa gur bhinne leo
chluinstin sa chruinniú,
Nó 'n píobaire 'seinm ó mhaidin go neoin.

A handsome young fellow, lissom and graceful,
I caught the girls' eyes wherever I went.
I'd coax them and kiss them.
I'd step down their road.
I'd treat them all 'dacint', left never a moan.
Each lass's bright eyes would
light up with pleasure;
Their cheeks all a-beam
with delight that I'd come.
And my voice, singing on,
in all company's delight,
Was sweeter than the piper playing all day.

Curfá

Och! Och! ar a' lá sin, murab é bhain a' bláth díom;
Sé d'fhág mé mar tá mé 'mo chréatúir gan dóigh.
Sé chlaoígh mé, sé chráidh mé,
gur chaolaigh mo chnámha;
Is d'fhág meath ar mo shláinte
nach léigheastar go deo.

Chorus

Woe for that day that
stole off my bloom;
Left me now a miserable mess.
It beat me and thrashed me,
till my brittle bones shook;
And rotted my health so I'll never improve.

2.

Ach anois iarraim párdún go léir ar na stáid-mhná.
Bhí cinealta cairdeach liom lá breá den tsaol.
Ná táthar a' rá liom gur dámnaithe atá mé;
Is nach dual domh go brách dhul
go flaithis na naomh.
Ach go n-admhaím, a Dhia,
go mbfhearr liom go síorruí,
Bheith i n-ifreann na bpían
i measc cáirde mo chléibh;
Ná bheith i bhflaithis in airde
'measc tuaitíní cráifeach';
Nach dtuigfeadh a' cás a d'fhág mise faoi léan.

But now I seek pardon of all these fair beauties,
Who were kind and so friendly once on a day.
For now it's said of me that
I'm damned down for ever;
And never to the saints' heaven
will I make my way.
But I beseech you, my God, that I'd far rather be
Stuck far down in hell with my own bosom pals
Than be in heaven above
with pious dullards for ever,
Who couldn't even understand
what has left me in thrall.

Curfá

Chorus

CHAPTER SIX

Songs of Tyrone

Though many a city since then I've been in,
New York, Chicago, Fort Wayne and Troy,
My heart still pines for your fields, Killeenan;
My bosom yearns for you, sweet Pomeroy.

SWEET POMEROY

As will become evident from the prosody, this village-name is two-syllabled. Locally it is even 'Primroy'. Over a hundred years ago, in the hilly village of Tyrone's Pomeroy, a friendly Orangeman warned Paddy Keenan's brother – Paddy it was who told me some three score years on – that if their cousin P.J. didn't clear out that night, he was for 'lifting' the next morning. So off he made for Queenstown and New York. Hard up there, he wandered down town. There he saw an Irish name above a shop. He took careful note of the whole shop-window. He wrote one of his usual poems and got it put in a local paper, as was his wont at home. 'When the owner saw the verses, he sent his aide-de-camp to offer P.J. a job. He got on great, finishing up as Superintendent of Customs at New York's docks.' He was buried at Calvary cemetery there in June 1926. 'Easter Sunday's Musings' by Felim O Dowd, his *nom de plume,* appeared in the *New York Daily News,* April 1891.

Sweet Pomeroy

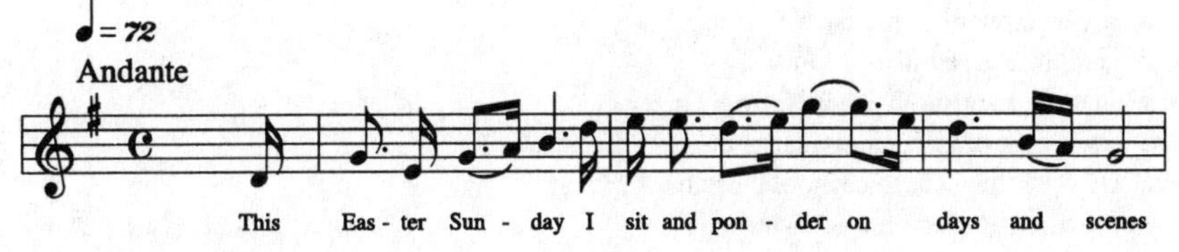

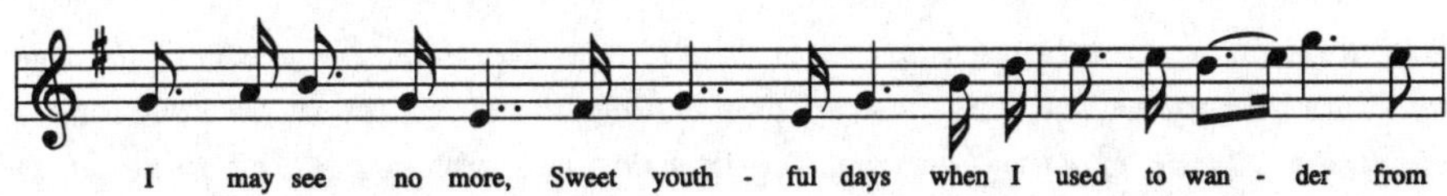

1.

This Easter Sunday I sit and ponder
On days and scenes I may see no more;
Sweet youthful days when I used to wander
From Cornamaddy to Carrickmore.
Though many a city since then I've been in,
New York, Chicago, Fort Wayne and Troy,
My heart still pines for your fields, Killeenan;
My bosom yearns for you, sweet Pomeroy.

Apt picture in the 1980s as a full century ago P.J. Fox showed here that American city names could meld just as featly as did the loved townlands at home. Hilaire Belloc says somewhere that this knack of garnishing verses with local place-names was the mark of a true poet. Much nearer to us today, John Betjeman had a helter-skelter tour of Ireland, using place-names lavishly, lovingly.

2.

A village perched on an elevation,
A murmuring streamlet that bathes its feet.
A lordly hall in a green plantation,
And a big wide fairground where farmers meet.
Three streets that branch from a large quadrangle;
A kirk, church, chapel and a school close by.
A little courthouse where lawyers wrangle;
And a neat post office – and that's Pomeroy.

Schooling? There was a hedge-school up to the 1914-18 war time. The master of the town school, Sean Anderson, had been a pupil of the hedge-school master in the townland of Turnabarson, Master Hagan. The scholars performed his farm chores first thing in the morning. The lessons came later. If they had nothing for the master in recompense, that was of no consequence. They had put in his crop for him.

3.

'Twas there I got what I have of schooling,
God bless the Master if he's living yet.
'Twas there I first met young Kitty Doolin,
And fell in love with her the hour we met.
Dear native hills, while the sky's above you,
While big Slieve Gallen lifts his crest on high,
While your waters flow to Lough Neagh, I'll love you;
My blest, my beauteous, my own Pomeroy.

Another product of Master Hagan's classical academy, John Matthew Quin, was to become the late Cardinal Ó Fiaich's second last Vicar-General, and Dean of the Dungannon deanery.

In 1978 I said, slowly enough for the old cleric:

'Dean, in three weeks' time, on RTÉ's 'Trom agus Éadtrom', I am going to sing for you what I sang for you and your 91-year-old father, in Pomeroy itself in 1951.'

Dean Quin loved this next verse.

4.

How sweet it was when my work was over,
To take a stroll round the sandy brae,
Where the corncrake craked in the dewy clover,
And the blackbird warbled his evening lay.
Beside me Kitty with her form so slender,
Her ripe red lip and her soft brown eye.
Arrah, what cared I about foreign splendour,
My El Dorado was sweet Pomeroy.

5.
Dear village, blest by the smiles of heaven;
With your nice white chapel and its soft-toned bell,
That used to summon to prayer the living,
And greet the dead with its parting knell.
Ah! would my ears could but hear it tolling,
'Twould fill my bosom again with joy.
But ah! the mighty Atlantic's rolling
Its waves 'twixt me and my own Pomeroy.

6.
And yet, who knows? I am not despairing;
If God so wills, I'll retread the scene.
I'll feast my eyes on the hills of Erin,
And see her Senate in College Green.
My arms will clasp forms 'twas death to sever,
Forms not beheld since I was a boy.
And when life's journeying is o'er for ever,
My place of rest may be sweet Pomeroy.

Ave atque vale. Salute P.J. Fox (Felim O Dowd), Bard of Gortnagarn.

THE HAWK AND THE CROW

I always found Tyrone a seed-bed for good local singers and songs.

John Francis Clarke and Phil Carberry sang at céilidhs in the old schoolhouse neighbouring mine at Altmore. Phil was a delight; shy enough to face diagonally into the wall, clutching his cap as he sang, he or John F., of Barberry Allen and the 'sail-i-or who fancied I'. But the palm goes to Phil's pair of lovebirds.

I called to visit poor John Francis perchance some few months before he died in late 1997 – good rest to him. He assured me that it was his old friend, Phil Carberry, and not himself, as I had thought, who sang 'The Hawk and the Crow' for me, all that half-century ago. They were both bonny singers.

In Peter Kenedy's *Folksongs of Britain and Ireland* (Oak Publications, London/New York/Sydney/Cologne, 1975-1984), p. 675, he notes that he and Sean O Boyle heard this song from me in 1953. He states 'generally known as "The Bird's Courting Song", this version of the song had not been noted in the British Isles until it appeared in Northern Ireland. It was therefore of great interest to come across a version still being sung in its country of origin before its flight across the Atlantic. In both the United States and in Ireland it was regarded as a children's song.' I'd dispute this. They'd be old-fashioned children! In those days particularly.

The Hawk and the Crow

1.

Said the Hawk unto the Crow one day,
'Why do you in mourning stay?'
'I was once in love and I didn't prove fact.
And ever since I wear the black.'

Chorus

Singing right a diddle, right a diddle,
right a diddly dum.
Singing right a diddle, right a diddle,
right a diddly dum.
'I was once in love and I didn't prove fact.
And ever since I wear the black.'

2.

Then up spoke the Willie Wagtail,
'I was once in love and I did prevail.
I was once in love and I did prevail.
And ever since I wag my tail.'

Chorus

3.

Next up spoke the little Brown Thrush;
She was singing in yon holly bush.
'The way to court, I've heard them say,
Is to court all night and sleep the next day.'

Chorus

4.

And last there spoke the Jenny Wran:
'Do you know what I'd do, if I was a man?
For fear that one would wriggle and go,
I would wear two strings unto my bow.'

Chorus

CARMIN FAIR

Saucy enough 'carry-on' a century and more past. Barely credible, though. Carrickmore folk once were a little, well less or more, put out at Pomeroy's gibes. Good friends always, though. Apprentice fiddlers used the melody, otherwise 'The Spanish Lady', for their early scraping. Carmin, the local version of Carrickmore, from the ancient name, Tearmon Mag Uirc (the sanctuary land of MacGurk).

1.

One very pleasant summer's morning,
When everything was bright and gay,
The birds sang out their songs most charming,
And I myself was as glad as they.
I dressed myself in my Sunday suit;
I washed my face and combed my hair.
I greased my brogues and sallied out,
For to spend the day at Carmin Fair.
Ho! Whack fol the tooral ooral addy!
Whack fol the tooral ooral ay!
Whack fol the tooral ooral addy!
Whack fol the tooral ooral ay!

2.

When I arrived at the town of Carmin,
Crowds of people thronged the street.
Some were dressed in silk and satin;
Some wore big brogues upon their feet.
Some had hankies round their heads,
With their legs and feet completely bare.
Such an awkward squad I ne'er did see,
As I met that day in Carmin Fair.

Whack fol...

3.

As I was passing them by in masses,
Examining them as I went along,
Looking at their fancy dresses,
I spied a maid among the throng.
Her cheek was fair, her figure neat,
And grand was the dress that she did wear.
I thought there was no one there that day,
To compare with her in Carmin Fair.

Whack fol...

4.

I invited her in to have a 'trate'
And she agreed without a frown.
So off we went with one consent,
To an alehouse up in Carmin town.
I called in a pint of good strong sherry,
And down in a snug armchair we sat.
Us two became both blithe and merry;
I counted myself a lucky brat.

Whack fol...

5.

When in my arms I held her folded,
And tasting her lips as I thought no sin;
The door at once became unbolted,
And a big rough man came stepping in.
Says he, 'Ye damned infernal ruffian!
How dare you so treat my wife?'
He began to give me such a 'batin',
That I almost thought he would take my life.

Whack fol...

6.

'Oh, husband dear, bate him well,' says she;
'He kissed me, squeezed me and tore my hair.'
Faith, he made me pay well for the day,
That I spent with his bride in Carmin Fair.
All you young lads that want a wife,
Of unknown females do beware.
Mind the disgrace that happened to me,
In that damned deceitful Carmin Fair.

Whack fol...

Two more for Carmin and for the Bard of Gortnagarn!

THE CREGGAN WHITE HARE

On the lowlands of Creggan there lies a white hare;
She's as swift as the swallow that flies through the air.
You may travel the country and find none to compare,
With the pride of low Creggan, the bonny White Hare.

Through this song or because of it I came to know, albeit for all too brief a time, Peter Padhra Ban Donnelly. The O'Donnellys were hereditary sub-chiefs of the great O'Neills of Dungannon and Tullyhogue. Almost in view of our school was a dip in the Sperrins called Shan Bearnagh's Chair, Shane or Seán Bearnach (John the Gapped). His great gapped mouth; no teeth ever; so hard that he was reputed to bite through thin plates of iron. That's where his lieutenants in the 1700s kept a sharp lookout for oncoming stage-coaches, to rob and plunder them.

A full two hundred and more years later; a hard frosty night, December 1951. Young master led to the slaughter.

'What age would you be now, Peter?'

'That same "questkin" was put to me in Belfast where I was giving word of mouth evidence about a "right of way".'

'How old are you, Mr Donnelly?'

'Well, your worship, last year I was 90, singing on the BBC. This year I am 91. In the High Coort in Belfast. Where the hell will I be next? "Do you know what I'm going to tell you?" says Judge Fox. "Yirr the best crack ivver sat in that box."'

Peter nearly floored the young contender with his opening: 'Morrisey and the Rooshin Sailor'; 38 rounds, bareknuckle fight; one verse to each round. Only faltering a very little in the 'thirties' verses. Tea and buns and 'sanngwidges' for all as an interval to the singing/caterwauling.

Then up speaks young Napoleon,
and takes his mother by the hand,
Saying, 'Mother dear, be patient
until I'm able to take command;
And I'll raise a mighty army
and through tremendous dangers go;
And I never will return again
till I've conquered the Bonny Bunch of Roses, O.'

On with the singing. Only occasional reels, jigs and hornpipes – very rarely a march, here as so often, alas – from the fiddlers who had brought me there: Paddy Nugent, Paddy Keenan and Tom MacElhatton in Gerard Clarke's car.

Call of nature. Relieving in a henhouse/cowbyre. Coming out, offered what looked like a watery substance in a sauce-bottle. 'No, thanks.' Finally, come 4.30 and time for home. Young contender, hoarse, exhausted, sung out.

Old champ, still hunched at table over his blackthorn stick, duncher-cap pushed back from victorious brow. Singing away!

'Saft' me. He sang on 'potchin' while I sang on 'tay'.

The Creggan White Hare

1.

On the lowlands of Creggan there lies a white hare;
She's as swift as the swallow that flies through the air.
You may travel the country and find none to compare
With the pride of low Creggan, the bonny White Hare.

2.

Till one fine Autumn morning as you might suppose,
As the red golden sun o'er the green valley rose,
Barney Conway came down and this did declare:
'This day I'll put an end to the Creggan White Hare.'

3.

He searched through the lowlands and down through the glens,
And among the green rushes where the White Hare had dens.
Till at last coming home on a bog bank so bare,
From behind a white thistle out jumped the White Hare.

4.

Bang! went his gun, and his dog he slipped too.
Across the green meadows like the March wind they flew.
But the dog soon came back, which made poor Barney cry.
For he knew that the White Hare had bid him goodbye!

5.

We had some jolly sportsmen down here from Pomeroy,
Cookstown, Dungannon and also the Moy.
With their pedigree greyhounds they came from afar;
And they travelled to Creggan in a fine motorcar.

6.

'Twas down through the lowlands the huntsmen did go;
To search for the White Hare they tried high and low.
Till at last Barney Conway, who came on its lair,
Shouted out to the sportsmen, 'Here lies your White Hare!'

7.

They called in the greyhounds from off the green lea,
And Barney and the huntsmen they jumped high with glee.
'Twas on a turfbank they all gathered round,
Seven men and nine dogs did the White Hare surround.

8.

No wonder the poor hare did tremble with fear,
As she stood on her toes she would raise a big ear.
But she stood on her toes and with one gallant spring
Jumped over the greyhounds and broke through the ring.

9.

The chase it went on, 'twas a beautiful view.
Across the green meadows like that March wind they flew.
But the pedigree greyhounds, they didn't go far.
They came back and went home in their fine motorcar.

10.

So now to conclude and to finish my rhyme;
I hope you'll excuse me for wasting your time.
If there's any among you in Carrickmore Fair,
Drink a jolly good health to the Creggan White Hare.

THE RAKE OF CARNTEEL

Now we encounter a self-centred rake: no more than a Don Giovanni does he feel abashed by the bold deeds he confesses. Carnteel is only a little village in Tyrone but it is linked with this rollicking song of a jack-of-all-trades.

Ar Tharraingt Siar go Carn Tsíail Domh

(Ar Harringt Shear Guh Karn Tail Doo)

THE RAKE OF CARNTEEL

1.

Ar tharraingt siar go Carn tSíail domh
An t-aonach céanna úd na Féil' Muire Mór;
Sé tharla an ainnir as an taobh aniar dom,
Is í go cianmhar ag siúl sa ród.
Is é níor mheas mé gur scar mo chíall uaim,
Mar bhínn ag síabhrán nó seal ag ól;
Óir tóigeadh domsa gur dhorcha an ghrian gheal,
Le taobh gach dealraimh d'a grua mar rós.

This rustic Casanova travels the whole northern half of our country, wenching, wassailing and working betimes. He not only kisses but tells, whether believed or not. Coming from his own Tyrone village, Carnteel, at the Lady Day Fair he met such a dazzling beauty that she left him crazed.

2.

Bheannaíos féin go prap don mhaighdean;
Is ní go séimhi ghlac crith mo ghlór.
D'fhiosraíos féin dí de fhearaibh Éireann,
An nglacfadh sí raoghain orm ins an ród.
Cheasnaigh sise díom cá raibh mo léine,
Mo bhuig, mo bhéabhar, gan fiú na mbróg?
'S'annamh chonaiceas sac mar éideadh
Ar fhear ag bréagadh na gcailín óg.'

When I put it to the lassie who best she'd favour, she
retorted that a shoeless, shirtless, wigless, hatless swain,
clad in his sack, would win no young maid.

3.

Ar an neamhchead dom shacán cnáibe,
Mo shean-triús Spáinneach, is mo bhoinéad ciar,
Is ró-maith aithnim idir an dubh is an bán;
's ní h-í an bhean is áilne is troime ciall.
Ná síl gur chugatsa atáim á rá sin,
A ainnir áluinn is finne ciabh;
Ach sílidh an iomad acu mé bheith i ngrá leo,
's is ró-bheag m'aird ar a leath nó a dtrian.

Whatever about my beggarly outfit, sackcloth,
old dark bonnet and all, I'm still no mug.
Don't feel that I'm only deceiving your lovely self.
Too many think I love them; poor fools.

4.

Bím go h-aerach ar mhalaidh shléibhe,
Ag déanamh bhéarsai is ag ceartú ceoil;
Seal ag pléideáil le mnáibh ar aontaíbh,
'gus seal ag bréagadh na gcailín óg.
Seal mo úcaire 'gus seal mo mhéire,
Mo bhuachaill spéire i dtigh an óil
Seal mo thunnadóir ag cartadh léabach
Idir an Éirne 's an Mullach Mór.

Whiles I be on the mountainside singing and making verses;
Whiles teasing women at fairs or deluding young girls. Times
I've been a fuller, a ganger, a dab in the pub; a tanner, a
pelt-stripper from the Erne to Mullaghmore.

5.

Bhí me i nDoire's me ag déanamh brící;
's i mBaile Uí Mhaoláin ag briseadh cloch;
In Inis Eoghain seal mo fhíodoir;
Is lán na míosa 'mo dhuine bhocht.
I mBaile an Mhullaigh ag teach aníos dom
Shuíos sios agus d'ólas deoch.
Bhí me i mBruíon Channain teacht na h-oíche,
Idir Ánna's Bríd is iad ag cíoradh folt.

On he traverses, temporary-jobbing; brickmaking, stone-
breaking, weaving; still a poor man, still tippling.
Nightfall he was there between Anna and Bríd as they did their
hair. All places from Hell to Connacht, one might say, in the
northern half from Dublin to Derry.

6.

Bhí mé ar an Mhuine Mhór is i gCaisleán Cába;
I mBaile Uí Dhalaigh is i Lios na Sciath;
Bhí me i Muineachán agus ar an Ghráinsigh;
Is ag Droichead Chúil Áine le corradh is bliain.
Aréir a tharlaidh i nDroichead Átha mé,
's anocht atá mé fá Charn tSíail.
's anois más roghain leat ar fhearaibh Fáil mé,
Seo mo lámh duit, bíom ag triall.

I've been to Moneymore; to Cape's Castle; to Ballygawley and Lisnaskea.
I was in Monaghan and the Grange; in Coolanny Bridge for a year and more.
Last night in Drogheda; tonight in Carnteel. (The wheel swings back.)
So, if you still choose me over the pick of all Ireland's men; I'm game.
Here's my hand! Off we go.

CHAPTER SEVEN

Some Great Slow Airs

W.B. Yeats once said of William Carleton, 1794-1869: 'His clay-cold melancholy; a great Irish historian; the great novelist of Ireland by right of the most Celtic eyes that ever gazed from under the brows of a story-teller.' Benedict Kiely, in his definitive study of Carleton, *The Poor Scholar*: (Carleton's mother): 'She sang as Irish women had sung for centuries before: with a voice rounded and sweet almost beyond human sweetness, a voice simple and untrained and unaffected, each line of Gaelic vibrant with trills and melodious grace-notes, the body rocking gently to and fro . . . The songs his mother sang were beautiful. The language in which those songs were written was, by association, beautiful. He remembered the day when she had grudgingly consented to sing an English version of "The Red-haired Man's Wife". She said the English words and the air were like a man and his wife quarrelling; the Irish words melted into the music.' (p 17)

The ballad-singer at the fair in the last century had no inhibitions as we may have today in 'Englishing' the lyrics.

THE RED-HAIRED MAN'S WIFE

Ye muses divine, combine and lend me your aid;
Till I pen these few lines for I find
my heart is betrayed,
By a maiden most fair who is dear to me as my life.
For from me she has flown and is known
as the red-haired man's wife.

A message I'll send by a friend down to the seashore;
To let her understand I'm the man
who does her adore.
And if she would but leave that slave I'd forfeit my life.
She'd live like a lady and ne'er be
the red-haired man's wife.

Seán Bán, *seanchaí* and poet, told that without the story behind it, the song was as orphaned as the pearl without a piece of black velvet to point up its lustre. Our song is no simple tale of lust. Fair lad and red-head were apprentices to the rich tailor. His only daughter and the fair lad were in love, betrothed to be married. (Of course, the storyteller, an albino, was an unprejudiced witness to the true story!) The foxy boy stole some silver knives of the tailor's and hid them in his rival's baggage. Discovered. Three years in gaol. Came out to find his love married to the rogue.

There you have it.

Bean an Fhir Rua

(Bann an Yirr Roo-ah)

THE RED-HAIRED MAN'S WIFE

1.

Is táilliúr beag aerach mé' déanamh éadaí
i dtí an fhir rua.
Nó go dtug mo chroí spéis dá béilín meala
gan ghruaim.
Agus thug mo chroí spéis dá béilín ba bhinne
nó 'n chuach.
'S a charaid mo chléibh dá n-éalótha liom
ó 'n fhear rua.

I'm a lively wee tailor at my trade
in the red-haired man's house.
My heart was enthralled with her
honey-sweet mouth, never glum.
And my heart was enthralled with her mouth;
no cuckoo more sweet.
And my heart's own darling,
leave the red-haired man for me.

2.

Is a bhruinneal gan smál 'bhfuil na
dealraitheacha deasa 'do ghrua;
Fá'n ógánach bhán atá cráite
le fada 'do dhiaidh.
Ní cheilim ar aoinneach cé an fáth
a bhfuil ormsa gruaim;
Dh'aoinneoin eaglais is bráithre sí
grá mo chroí bean an fhir rua.

And my peerless maid with
your shining lovely looks;
Of the fair-haired lad who has
pined for you many a year.
I conceal it from none why
my woe is heavy and sore;
In spite of church and friars my heart's
love is the red-haired man's wife.

3.

Tá crann sa gharrdha a bhfásann
air an bláth buí;
Is nuair a leagaim mo lámh air
is láidir go scoilteann mo chroi.
Is ní iarrfhainn aon achuinge ar
Ard-Rí na bhflaitheas anuas;
Ach an aon phóg amháin a fháil
ó bhean an fhir rua.

There's a tree in the garden whose blossom
blooms glowing and gold.
When I lay my hand on it my heart
is shattered, is cold.
I'd ask no request of the High King
in Heaven above;
But for one little kiss, just the one
from the red-haired man's wife.

4.

Dá gcuirtí mé síos i bpríosún
dhubh dhorcha chruaidh;
Na boltái bheith ar mo chaolchorp
'sna mílte glas ó sin suas.
D'éireoinn de rúchladh mar a
d'éireodh an eala den chuan;
Ar acht a bheith sínte seal oíche
le bean an fhir rua.

If I were to lie in a prison
black dark and grim,
With manacles biting my thin shanks,
with manifold chains,
I'd leap with a spring like the swan
zooming up from the sea;
To lie for one night in bed
with the red-haired man's wife.

THE NOBLE HILL OF KANEBECANTY

The best university lecturer ever I had – well, one of the best – was Daniel Corkery. He nurtured two great writers in Cork, Frank O'Connor and Séan Ó Faoláin. Greatly influenced by his seminal book on the great Munster Gaelic poets of the eighteenth century, *The Hidden Ireland,* was also a fine modern Gaelic poet, Seán Ó Ríordáin. Fully entitled to rank in that august company is our Belfast master, principally of the short story like O'Connor, but also a fine novelist, Michael Mac Laverty. He hastened to acknowledge his fealty to Corkery's literary philosophy.

And yet, and yet, Corkery in his *Hidden Ireland* made an egregious blunder. He referred to the 'minor Gaelic poets of South-East Ulster'. In fully as seminal a book of literary merit as Corkery's, in possibly his book that will outlast in the coming century any other Gaelic writer, Seosamh Mac Gríanna in *Padraic Ó Conaire agus Aistí Eile* sets the record straight. I repeat again that this *Padraic O'Conaire and Other Themes* is a major book of percipient criticism. It must be allowed that Corkery's *Hidden Ireland* is another such landmark in our literature. Seosamh Mac Gríanna opined that Ó Doirnín's great love-poem on *The Noble Hill of Kanebecanty* is as mellifluous and as skilfully wrought as any in modern Irish prosody.

Úr-Chnoc Chéin Mhic Cáinte

(Ure Knuck Kane Vick Canty)

The Noble Hill of Kanebecanty

A day of great moment, 1969, when on Killen Hill, just over the Louth border from South Armagh, I had the distinction of leading some hundreds of *Éigse Oirialla* members and friends in singing this song. Máirtín Ó Cadhain, a major writer of our time, was there and, doughty '*laoch*' as he was, was moved to tears by the fitting memorial to the little schoolmaster. How many of today's poets, in Irish or English, will be so celebrated in the year 2195? In the poem, the poet and the 'fuller' MacArdle of Culloville were in bardic contention for who would win the beautiful girl by the power of his poesy. Peadar Ó Dubhda, musician, playwright, broadcaster, and splendid singing teacher in Gaeltacht

Colleges in Rann na Feirste and Ó Meith Mara, Co. Louth, supplied the music. Unconsciously enough, as the scholarly Br O Caithnia avers, he 'composed' the melody to fit Ó Doirnín's words; genuinely oblivious of the melody collected by himself in the Omeath Gaeltacht in County Louth.

1.

A chiúin-bhean tséimb na gcuachann péarlach,	O gentle maiden of the lustrous locks,
Gluais liom féin ar ball beag;	come off with me a little,
Nuair a bhéas uaisle is cléir is tuataí i néall,	When lords and clerics are sound asleep,
In a suan faoi éadaí bána.	beneath sheets so snowy white.
In uaimh go mbéinn i bhfad uafa 'raon,	In a cave we'd be far off alone when
Teach nua-cruth gréine amárach.	dawn comes flooding tomorrow.
Gan ghuais linn féin i n-uaigneas aerach	And no fort 'neath the sun will be nearly as
San uaimh sin Chéin Mhic Cáinte.	snug as the airy hollow of Kanebecanty.

A scholarly Church of Ireland Canon of Saint Patrick's (Dean Swift's) Cathedral, Dublin, Canon Coslett Quin, took me to one side at an Éigse (Gaelic literary festival), and tutored me in the vowel sounds peculiar to the area. The Canon was an acknowledged authority on the Gaelic of South Armagh.

2.

A rún mo chléibh nach mar súd a bhféarr duit,	My heart's delight, would it not please you more
Tús do shaoil a chaitheamh liom?	To commence your life with me?
Is gan bheith i gclúid faoi léan ag búr gan chéill,	And not be stuck in a corner with this senseless boor,
I gcionn túirne is péire cártaí.	Attending your wheel and the carding-pairs.
Gheobhair ciúl na dtéad le lúth na méar,	You'll have stringed strains played with fingers so apt
Do do dhúscadh is bhéarsaí grá.	To awaken you, and loving verses.
'S níl dún faoi 'n ghréin chomh súgach aerach	And no fort 'neath the sun is so airy and sweet
Le h-Úr-Chnoc Chéin Mhic Cáinte.	As the Noble Hill of Kanebecanty.

3.

Táim brúite i bpian gan suan gan néall,	I'm sorely in pain, with neither wink or sleep,
De do chumha-sa, a ghéag is áilne.	In grief for you, my bloom so lovely.
Is gur tú mo roghain i gcúigibh Éireann,	And you my choice throughout all Ireland,
An chúis nach séanaim áthas de.	That's why I deny not my joy.
Dá siúlfá, a réalt gan smúid, liom féin	Should you walk, my flawless star, with me
Ba súgach saor ár sláinte,	How hale and free we should be.
Gheofa plúr is méad is cnuasacht craobh	You'd receive flour and mead and fruits galore
sa dún sin Chéin Mhic Cáinte.	In that forth of Kanebecanty.

THE BROWN SLOEBUSH

D.B: 'This is a great melody with beautiful construction.'

Some years ago the late Johnny Doherty, superb Donegal fiddler, one of four gifted brothers, made the far from bombastic claim: 'Our people have been playing this music since the princes had their castles in Donegal.' Again, the maestro, Seán Ó Riada, referred to *Ceol na nUasal.* He had in mind for this princely music such gems as this 'Brown Sloebush'. The savant, Br Liam Ó Caithnia, after years of fruitless research, is convinced that our great slow airs, such as any baroque composer might have been proud to claim, were composed not by any acknowledged composers but by the *'cos-mhuintir'*, the common people. With the breakdown of the old Gaelic order, they savoured and cherished their majestic melodies.

Let future research tell us otherwise.

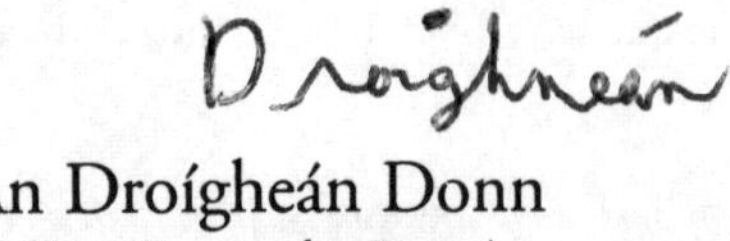

An Droígheán Donn

(Ann Dree-nahn Dunn)

THE BROWN SLOEBUSH

♩= 72
Andante

1.

Sílidh céad acu gur leo féin mé
nuair a ólaim leann;
Théid dhá dtrian síos díom nuair a
smaoítim ar a gcomhrá liom,
Sneachta séidte is é a shíor-chur
ar Shliabh Uí Fhloinn;
Is go bhfuil mo ghrá-sa mar bhláth
na n-áirní ar an Droighneán Donn.

A hundred of them think they own me
when I drink their ale.
Most of them would consort with me
if I believe what they say.
My love is lovelier far than the driven snow
on the mountain of O'Flynn;
And she's only to be compared with the
tender blooms on the Brown Sloebush.

Next, we meet a well-worn conceit, perhaps, but sweetly expressed.

2.

Fear gan chéill é 'bheadh a' dréim
leis a' chraoibh 'tá ard;
Is a' crann beag íseal le na thaobh-sa
ar a leagfadh sé a lámh.
Cé gur ard a' crann caorthainn
bíonn sé searbh as a bharr;
Is fásaidh sméara 's bláth sú-chraobh
ar a' chrann is ísle bláth.

Only the fool strives to climb
to the topmost bough,
With there beside him a little low tree
that can be easily reached.
The rowan tree grows high and fine,
but his fruit at the top is sour.
While blackberries and raspberries
grow on the lowest bough.

3.

Dá mbéinn 'mo bhádóir ba deas a
shnámhfainn 'n fharraige seo anonn.
Dá mbeadh léigheann agam scríofainn
líne le barr mo phinn.
Mo léan géar gan mé 's tú
a phógfadh mo bhéal
I ngleanntáin tsléibhe le h-éirí gréine
's a' driúcht 'na luí.

If I were a boatman I'd readily
sail to you across the sea.
If I were a scholar I'd write you
a line with a ready pen.
Oh! my misfortune that I'm not with you
who would kiss my mouth,
In a mountain valley, while the
morning dew lies thickly around.

In this final verse of an All-Ireland great slow air, such as Willie Clancy had in mind, the great scholarly singer, friend and mentor to me, Hughie Phaddy O'Devanney, emphasised to me how keen he was to acknowledge its probable Munster provenance. Hence, the warm Munster vocables.

Labhraim = I speak. *meabhrú* = thinking.
domhain = deeply.

4.

Má thig tú choíche
tar san oíche go cúl a' tí;
Tráthnóna nó go moch ar maidin
nuair bíos a' driúcht 'na luí.
Cé nach labhraim bím a' meabhrú
go domhain fá mo chroí;
Is tú mo cheadsearc agus ní
féidir mo chumha chlaoi.

Should you come, come at night
to the rere of the house;
In the evening or at early morn
with the dew still around.
Though I don't speak still I ponder
so deeply in my heart;
You're my only love and
nothing can overcome my woe.

DARK MOLLY OF THE GLEN

'Moll Dubh' or again 'Bean Dubh a' Ghleanna' ('Dark Moll'/'Woman of the Glen') is one of the great slow airs that tax the playing of the best of instrumentalists. Willie Clancy yearned to be able to sing it.

Let Moll speak for herself; or rather let her suitor tell us of her.

Moll Dubh a' Ghleanna

(Mahl Doo A Ghlanna)

DARK MOLLY OF THE GLEN

1.

Ag Moll Dubh a' ghleanna atá mo ghrá le fada;
Sí nach bhfuair guth nó náire.
Is is múinte céillí cneasta dúirt sí liom ar maidin,
'Imigh is ná pill go brách orm.'
Níl ógánach gasta o Bhaile Átha Cliath
go Gaillimh,
Nó siar go hUmhaill Uí Mháille;
Nach mbeadh a' triall a' ghleanna
ar eachrai slime sleamhna;
Ag iarraidh ar Mholl Dubh le pósadh.

Dark Moll of the Glen has my constant true love.
She was never talked about nor scandalised.
Politely, urbanely she told me this morning,
'Be off, and don't come back again to me.'
Swains from every town, from Dublin
to Galway,
And over to Ooilleewallia,
Come riding up the glen on
their sleek, glossy steeds;
All seeking for Dark Moll to wed.

2.

Tá ba agam ar sliabh 's níl aon duine
agam na ndiaidh;
Agus tá mé mo chríathrú leofa.
A' seoladh soir is siar as achan áit
a mbíonn a dtriall;
's a n-aghaidh ar a bhaile tráthnóna.
Folamh liom féin óró feasta ní bhéinn,
Ach Moll Dubh bheith i dtús a h-óige;
Nuair a chríonas a' tslat ní bhíonn
uirthi tlacht,
Mar bíos ar na crannaibh óga.

I've cows on the moor and no one to tend them;
And I'm being ruined with them.
Driving east and west from
every airt they come;
And them heading home in the evening.
I'm dead set never again to be broke;
But to have Dark Moll in
the prime of her youth.
When the branch once hardens
it loses its suppleness;
As once when young trees bloomed.

3.

Dá bhfhaghainn-se bean an Impire,
bean Rí na Fraince,
Nó níon eile de chuid Rí Seoirse;
Bean na mbachall caoin a bhreoidh
go deo mo chroí;
Bean eile agus dhá mhíle bó léi.
Níon óg an Iarla is í bheith i bpriacal,
Is í a teacht ag iarraidh orm le pósadh;
Mná deasa' n domhain is iad ar mo roghain;
Sí Moll Dubh a' Ghleanna a phósfainn.

If I should get the Empress herself,
or even the Queen of France;
Again, say King George's daughter;
The lady with the comely curls
who ever wounded my heart;
Another lady with two thousand cows;
The Earl's daughter, too, even she is in peril,
Even she coming here to wed me;
All the beauties of the world, and they to be my choice;
Dark Moll of the Glen I'd wed there.

4

Siúd é thiar mo theach, níl tuí air no scráth;
'S é déanta ar leathaoibh a' bhóthair.
Is nach críonna 'n rud a' bheach
nuair a ní sí a nead,
I dteas agus i dtús an Fhómhair,
Is fann guth an éin a labhras leis féin,
Ar an tulaidh nó ar shliabh na móna.
Is é díobháil na bhfear a d'fhág sinn ar lár;
Agus scaoilimís ár mbeannacht leofa.

Over there's my house; neither
straw nor sods for roof;
Sitting there by the side of the road.
How cunning is the bee, when she builds her nest,
In the heat at the beginning of harvest.
How weakly croaks the bird out there all alone,
On the hillock or on the boggy mount.
And it's the scarcity of men that has us forlorn;
So here goes our blessing with them.

THE CHARISMATIC FATHER DONAL

It is a matter for chagrin that our Gaelic word *Oireachtas* is often explicable as our equivalent of the Welsh word *Eisteddfod.* In the cultural meaning it is the convocation each year of Gaelic speakers, pre-eminently from Gaelic-speaking areas – our Gaeltacht – to enjoy the best of our literature, music and song.

In 1980 at the *Oireachtas* singing competition for the coveted O'Riada Cup, a lady sang this song. Bríd Bean Uí Mhonacháin was in contention for a place but lost her nerve in the finals. Two of the adjudicators sought her out later, to hear more about the song.

She had heard it on old tapes in *Cumann Cluain Ard,* Belfast. Only a garbled version. In Rann na Feirste Seán Bán and his sister, Annie Bhán, racked their memories and gave her four rich verses. Rann na Feirste had the poetry but for once had missed out on this remarkable melody, sung by a remarkable ninety-year-old little woman, Síle Mhicí Uí Ghallchóir. Doncha Mac Fhionnlaich, T.D. for that Donegal area, was proud to speak to me of Síle, his great-grand-aunt.

The song tells, in the first verse only, of a remarkable friar, Father Donal. The richness of the language, even in this first verse, caused an acknowledged Gaelic scholar to almost leap from his chair, on its first hearing.

An Fhial-Athair Dónall

(Unn Fee-ahl Ah-irr Doh-nal)

THE CHARISMATIC FATHER DONAL

1.

Ra 'idh mise siar go mullach Shliabh an Fhiaigh,
Go bhfeice mé an Fial-Athair Dónall;
Is gur fuide liom nó bliain gach lá
go mbíom a' triall,
A' tarraingt ar an chliar mhódhmhar.
A ghnúis gheal nár fhiata, 'Úmhlaigh aniar'
'tá cumhdaithe de 'n chiall ró-mhaith;
Is is brúite i bpian tá a' chlúid seo 'do dhiaidh,
A' dúil leat gach aon oích' Dhomhnaigh.

I'll travel off west to the Raven's Mountain top,
'til I see the gracious Father Donal.
And each day on my way is longer than a year,
As I draw near to this lovely friar.
His beaming friendly face,
'Come over here, my dear,'
Suffused with wise counsel.
And how painful we feel in our own little spot;
Every Sunday night here we await you.

2.

I mBaile'n tSagairt tá'n dóigh gur
mhéanra bheith 'na chómhair;
B'fhurast bheith beo ar mhairtfheoil.
Bíonn imirt agus ól, aiteas agus spóirt;
Seinm agus ceol cláirsí.
An lil agus an rós i n-imill achan róid,
's an iomaite den phór garraí.
Dúshlán dá bhfuil beo nó marbh riamh go fóill,
Sneachta fheiceáil ann nó deor bháisti.

Ballintaggart is where you should surely be;
You'd never die for want of fresh beef.
They have card-playing, drinking,
crack and sport; musicking
And strumming on the harp.
The lily and the rose lining every road,
abundance of garden produce.
Live or dead we challenge if they ever did see
snow there or ever a raindrop.

3.

Nár mhéanra don té a tharlaigh in a léithéid,
ní fhásann an féar garbh ann.
Thig solus as a' spéir is dealramh ó'n ghréin,
agus ceoltaí ó thaobh na farraige.
I gcúplaí bíos cadhain, seabhach in a ndiaidh,
i ngleanntáin na séimh-sealga.
Is gurb é aireas a' chliar gurb e Párthas na Naomh é,
'gus ceolta na n-éan a gcealgadh.

How fortunate the man who happened on this place;
no trace of coarse grass around.
Light pouring from the sky, gleaming from the sun;
music in the air from the sea.
A brace of brent-geese, a hawk stalking them,
in the glens so rich in fine hunting.
And the clergy still aver, it's Saints' Paradise
for sure, as the warbling birds allure us.

4.

Siomaí abhaill chúmhra folaithe go dlúith,
agus coillte go h-úr a' fás ann.
Loingeas ar a' stiúir in a mbeirteanna 's 'na dtriúireanna,
A' tarraingt ar siúl adhmaid
Maise, fear as Cúige Mumhan a d'aithris dom faoí rún,
Gur bhreathnaigh sé na cúig ceárna;
Is nach bhfaca riamh a shúil in aon
bhealach in a shiúl,
A léitheid de chluain fhásaigh.

Many a fragrant grove, thickly concealed,
and coppices newly flourishing.
Vessels sailing by, twos and threes at a time,
coming to load up with timber.
Sure, a Munsterman confided to me,
he had travelled the five airts;
And nowhere had he seen
No matter where he went,
Any such well clothed meadow.

THE GATES OF ATHBOY

This is the rare tale of the Lothario being impotent because of drink. Back in the heroic saga tales, the valiant warrior after one lusty copulation was urged by his mate:

'Dein arís é.' 'Do it again.'
'Níl mé i ndán.' 'I'm not able.'

Impotent or otherwise, our boy left a lovely song.

Geaftaí Bhaile Áth' Buí

(Gaffitee Whella Bwee)

THE GATES OF ATHBOY

1.

Ag geaftaí Bhaile Atha Buí a rinne mise
'n gníomh a bhí amaideach baoth-dhéanta;
Éalodh le mnaoí seal tamaill 'san oích',
ar neamhchead a raibh faoí na spéartha.
Mar bhí mé óg gan bhrí,
gan mhisneach i mo chroí;
Is í agam ar mhín shléibhe.
Bhí a' codladh a' mo chlaoí,
is b'éigin dom-sa luí;
Is d'imigh sí 'n a fíormhaighdean.

By Athboy Town's gates I did the deed
that was foolish and feckless enough.
I slipped off with a lass for a while
of a night, with no heed to all and sundry.
Well, I was young and callow,
a craven in my heart;
here I had her on that brae side.
Sleep laid me low,
I had to stretch out;
and off she went still quite intact.

2.

A' gabháil a luí don ghréin a' t-am seo aréir,
nach agam bhí a' scéala buartha?
B'é a shamhailt dom a' té a shínfí sa chré,
is a Mhuire nach mé a' trua?
Sé deirfeadh mo chairde, a' méid acu
bhí i láthair,
'Altuigh leis ma mná, a bhuachaill.'
Is a' méad ghoillfeadh ortha mo chás,
ghoilfeadh siad a sáith,
Fá'n chroi bheith mo lár i na ghual dubh.

As the sun sank down this time last night
hadn't I enough to sadden me?
I was like someone stretched in the clay;
and oh! Mary, am I not the one to be pitied?
My friends would surely say,
those who stood around,
'Be thankful for all women, my lad.'
And those who were pained for my plight,
they would surely weep their fill
That my heart in my bosom is coal-black.

3.

Dá mbéinn thall sa Spáinn mo luí
ar leaba a' bháis;
Agus chluininn do dháil in Éirinn;
Go n-éireoinn chomh sámh leis
a' bhradán ar a' tsnámh;
I nduibheagán i lár na hÉirne.
Focal ar bith mná ní chreidfidh mé go brách,
Mura bhfeicfidh mé scríofa i mBéarla é;
Is gur chaith mé naoi lá 'cleasaíocht leis a' bhás,
I ndúil go bhfuíghinn spás ar éigin.

If I were there in Spain
stretched on my bed to die,
And I to hear you were to wed in Ireland;
I'd rise up smooth as the salmon
swimming away
In the depths of the River Erne.
A woman's word again I'll never ever trust,
Unless I see it written clearly in English;
And for nine days I've wrestled with very death itself,
Hoping for some respite to relieve me.

4.

Is agam tá a' mhaistreas
is measa i gCríochaibh Fáil,
Cé gur soineannta sámh a h-éadán.
Cuireann sí mo chás i bhfad agus i ngearr;
Ach b'fhurast ár gcás a réitiú.
An mada rua bheith sách, a' chaora dhubh ar fáil;
Is ni chluinfí mé go brách ag éileamh.
Is m'fhocal duit a Sheáin,
go bhfuil ealaíon ins na mná;
Agus codail fein go sámh 'n a n' éamuis.

My mistress is the stoniest all Ireland over;
Although her brow is innocent and guileless.
She scatters my love hither and thither;
But still we'd agree quite easily enough.
If the red fox were filled,
the black sheep to hand;
I'd never once be complaining.
And I tell you now, Sean,
that women are all guile;
And sleep the more soundly without them.

THE POET-RAPAREE

The poet-raparee (highwayman) Séamus MacMurchaidh (MacMurphy) was hanged outside Armagh Gaol some 200 years ago. He was a close friend of two better poets, Art Mac Cumhaidh and Peadar Ó Doirnín. His name may outlast theirs, unfairly perhaps, because of this song and of his tragic love for Malaidh Ní Dheacair (Molly Hardy). She the noted beauteous daughter of a covetous shebeen-keeper, Patsy. He the vainglorious six-feet-six-inches-tall raparee; loved by too many girls, to Molly's chagrin. Rash and dashing Séamus used to leap out before a stagecoach, with the clarion call, *'Mise Séamus 'ac Murchaidh is deise 'tá i n-Éirinn!'* 'Meet Jamesy MacMurphy, the handsomest in Ireland.' Talk of Mohammed Ali of the eighteenth century!

Nemesis finally caught him up. The notorious John Johnston, State head-hunter for these raparees, tempted Patsy with money to urge his jealous daughter to set a trap for her only love. Séamus's lieutenant, Arty Fearon, over-keen himself to win Molly, filled her with poisonous accounts of the giant's 'illicit loves'. She lured Séamus to a trysting at the Flagstaff Inn; damped the powder in his pistols while he lay in a drunken stupor. Johnston's soldiers seized him, brought him to Armagh where he was hanged.

Séamus 'Ac Murchaidh

(Shamus ak Murrcha)

SEAMUS MACMURPHY

He sings:

1.

Ar Mhullach Shliabh gCuilinn bhí an choirm a réidhtiú; Agus Séamus 'ac Murchaidh mar thaoiseach ar an fhéasta. Chá dtabharfadh sé urraim do bhodaigh an Bhéarla. Is tá sé inniu in Ard Mhacha is gan fáil ar a réidhtiú.	On the mount of Slieve Gullion the banquet was all arranged; And Seamus MacMurphy was leader of all. He would give no obeisance to the Saxon churls. Today he's in Armagh with no one to release him.

2.

Tá mé inniu in Ard Mhacha is is fuar liom mo ghéibheann. Siad mo chomharsain lucht mo chéasta is is nimh liom a bpléisiur. Ní thuigeann siad mo chanamhaint is chá labhraim leo Béarla; Ach sí m'annsacht an bhean dubh tá i ngleanntáin an tsléibhe.	Today in Armagh, my incarceration so cold. My cellmates torment me; to hell with their 'fun'. They know not my tongue, no English I'll speak; But my dear's the dark girl on the high glenside.

3.

Trua gan mé 'mo fhraochog ar thaobh mhalaí shléibhe; Nó 'mo shamharcán deas gréigeal ar dhéisiúr na gréine. Nó mar Shéamus 'ac Murchaidh is deise bhí in Éirinn; Agus dhéanfainn an Nollaig ar an Chreagán da bhféadfainn.	Alas I'm not a whortleberry on the mountainside; Or a pretty little primrose being gilt by the sun. Or still be Jamesy MacMurphy, the handsomest in Ireland; And I'd celebrate this Christmas in Creggan, if I could.

The quality of the verse rises so high that scholars deem that Ó Doirnín's hand shows in it. Peadar Ó Doirnín and indeed Art MacCooey and our MacMurphy were all disaffected members of a south Armagh fraternity, dispossessed and hounded by the notorious John Johnston. This same 'gentleman' of Roxborough House, near Newtownhamilton, was such a scourge to the countryside that his name is still recalled, two hundred years on. A neighbour lady declaimed to me:

Jesus of Nazareth, King of the Jews;
Save us from Johnston, Lord of the Fews.

Some twenty-eight verses in all, in an 'anthem sung widely from Blacksod to Carlingford', in the last century.

Nemesis for Séamus, but a name for posterity while grass grows and water flows and Gaelic mellifluously survives. Patsy, the covetous father, coming home the twenty-eight arduous miles from Armagh to the Flagstaff near Omeath, fell dead ascending the

Flagstaff's steep slope, carrying the twenty-five pounds 'blood money', doled out to him in small copper coins by the contemptuous soldiery. Arty, the treacherous lovelorn lieutenant, is waylaid and killed by others of Séamus's clan/gang, returning from the hanging.

Molly herself, forgiven in her lover's verse, is received in amity by the MacMurphy family, by her tragic lover's last wish, despite her treachery. But the popular song at wakes, weddings and all festive occasions, with its constant reminder of the handsome, forgiving suitor who died because of her, almost for her, led to her despairing leap to her death in a dark tarn (mountain lake).

The melody is one of many handed down, some not worthy of the theme. This one is also sung to lyrics of Ben Neifin in Mayo. Only two others of the many verses we recount here.

4.

Is a Mháilidh mhín mhómhar, má
d'órdaigh tú an bás domh;
Triall 'un mo thórraimb is
cóirigh faoi chlár mé.
Ma's mian leat mo phósadh is
mo chroí-se bheith ar láimh leat;
Pill arís is tabhair póg domb
is beidh do chroí-se lán-tsásta.

And my blithe, gracious Molly,
even if you did fix my death,
Come to my funeral and
dress me for the grave.
If you still wish to wed me,
with our hearts side by side,
Come back and kiss me and
your heart will be well pleased.

A fitting conclusion to our song. This verse in its last line, particularly, has been hailed by Séamus Ó Grianna as the most poignant in modern Gaelic letters.

5.

Triallfaidh mo thórramh
tráthnóna Dia h-Aoine,
Is ar maidin Dia Domhnaigh
fríd na bóithre gois íseal.
Tiocfaidh Neillidh agus Nóra
agus óg-mhná na tíre;
Is beidh mé ag éisteacht le na nglórthaí
faoi na fóide is mé sinte.

My cortège sets off
on next Friday evening;
And early on Sunday
by the low-lying roads.
There'll be Nellie and Nora
and all the young girls;
And I'll hear their voices,
'neath the sod where I lie.

CHAPTER EIGHT

Folk-Songs Nearer Home

An Ulsterman I am proud to be,
From Antrim's Glens I come.

Well, not wholly true. I was born in north Belfast, almost in the lea of Cave Hill. So, an Antrim man. But also, a citizen of 'no mean city'. Once when I quoted to an attendant at Belfast Central Railway Station that I was proud to say, 'I was born and bred in Belfast. Indeed, like Saint Paul of Tarsus, I was a citizen of "no mean city,"' he answered, 'Ah see yeh know yirr Bible, friend.' Herewith, an authentic folk-song written in this century.

A TRACE-BOY OF LIGONIEL HILL
My own father, good rest to him, often told of the horse-trams and the trace-horses held ready to give extra traction up the hilly roads like Cliftonville, Oldpark and 'all their daddies', Ligoniel.

'Boy, to see them trace-boys ride hell-for-leather down Cliftonpark Avenue on their way to the stables for the night was a sight for sore eyes. Talk about Cowboys and Indians!'

Fire-brigade engines were also horse-drawn. 'I seen them one night, wet and greasy on the "square-setts". Four massive horses, almost Clydesdales, lashed on to a reported blaze in Brookfield Mill. Not too far from the fire-station the whole "shebang" went skittering-skidding outside the main gate to Ardoyne Monastery chapel. The front-off one went down, struggled to rise. No chance. Back and one leg knocked out. "Not bummin' about it, boy; I was able to help pacify the poor baste." By this time a big RIC man on duty had waved down a baker's cart. Willy or nilly, the breadman's horse was untackled and joined the three intact horses. Off they went to their fire. All took longer to tell than to do.'

Hugh Quinn, the author of this authentic Belfast folk-song, was a fellow teacher in Saint Comgall's primary school, Belfast, in the early years of the 1939-45 War.

He had in mind for his melody a pert little Belfast street-song, which I often listened to in my very early years, as the 'wee girls' solemnly paraded, sometimes clad in cast-off grownups' finery, come the bright heartsome days of May.

Green Gravel, Green Gravel;
Your dress is so green.
You're the fairest young damsel
That ever was seen.
I washed her, I dressed her;
I robed her in silk;
And I wrote down her name
With a gold pen and ink.

If I have the good fortune to meet Hugh in the hereafter, I'll beg his indulgence for casting off his projected melody for my preference, adapted from a County Down folk-song:

A wee maid going to Comber,
Her market to 'larn';
To sell for her mammy
Some hanks of fine yarn.
She met with a young man
Upon the highway;
Which caused the wee damsel
To dally and stray.

We are assured by St John Ervine in a foreword to his *Mrs McConaghy's Money*, published by Constable, that Hugh was a gifted dramatist. Micheál MacLiammóir hailed it as the best play to come out of the North in those years before 1939. Hugh was a product of the not-to-be-derided 'monitor' system. He stayed on at Milford Street public elementary school having 'gone there as far as the master could put him'. For the next few years he was an unpaid 'apprentice' teacher, a monitor. Outside school, in those harsh days of the 'half-timers', he functioned as an unpaid 'schoolboord' to coax the children to school on the days, turn about, they were 'free' from the grinding linen mills. He could tell himself how a warm bond was established with parents and children. Very little money around but no shortage of goodwill. All weddings, wakes and christenings saw him as a welcome guest. He could recall clearly the country carts trundling in with bedding, sticks of furniture, maybe even 'a clatter of hens', as Tyrone and Armagh folk came seeking a living in 'black Belfast'.

A Trace-Boy of Ligoniel Hill

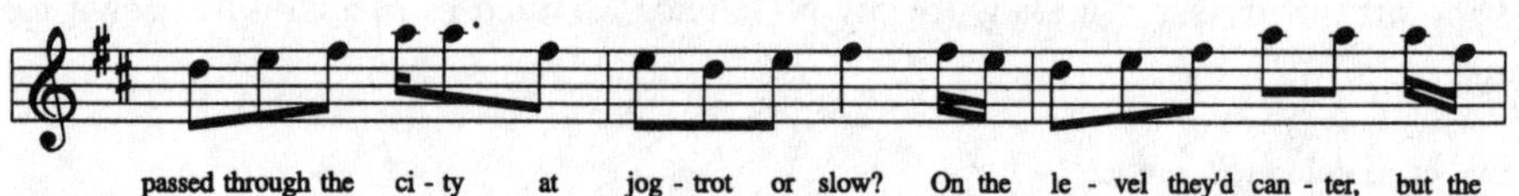

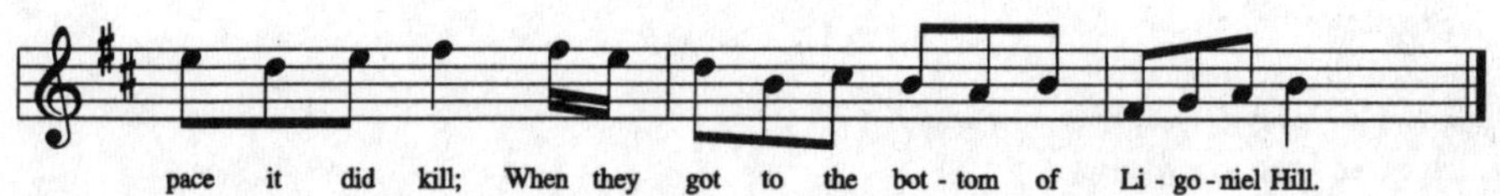

1.

Do you mind the old horse trams a long time ago;
As they passed through the city at jog-trot or slow?
On the level they'd canter but the pace it did kill;
When they got to the bottom of Ligoniel Hill.

2.

But the trace-boys were there with a heart and a hand;
They let down the traces and buckled each band.
The passengers sat on, contented and still,
When they saw the bold trace-boys of Ligoniel Hill.

3.

Away we did canter as fast as the wind,
And left the poor country carts plodding behind.
And that song of the wind in my ears I hear still;
As when I was a trace-boy on Ligoniel Hill.

4.

My friends all departed, and work now so scarce;
The only thing left is a ride in a hearse,
With the sky for my roof and my bed a brick-kiln.
Yet I once was a trace-boy on Ligoniel Hill.

THE MUTTONBURN STREAM

Archie MacCready used to promise me in Antrim, 'If you come with me some day, master, I can show you where the Muttonburn stream rises.' He spoke, too, of Ballyboley in that same area of the stream. When I reflect on Eric Bogle's harrowing anti-war song, 'And the Band Played Waltzing Matilda', I recall Antrim town, 7 June 1798. So many bodies were collected, after the militia's carnage in the town, that they were heaved into carts and piled out in mass graves on the sandy banks of the River Sixmilewater. An English army officer called out as he oversaw the horrible mess:

'Where are they all from?'

One wretch, skull almost split in two from a sabre slash, answered from the midst of the dead bodies covering him:

'Ahm frae Ballyboley.'

1.
I remember my young days;
Aye, for younger I've been.
I remember my young days,
By the Muttonburn Stream.
It's not marked on the world's map;
Nowhere to be seen,
A wee river in Ulster,
The Muttonburn Stream.

2.
Och, it flows under bridges,
Takes many's a turn.
Sure it turns round the millwheels
That grind the folks' corn.
And it ripples o'er meadows
And keeps the land clean.
Belfast Lough it soon reaches,
The Muttonburn Stream.

3.
The fine ladies of Carrick
I oft-times have seen,
Bringing down their fine washing
To the Muttonburn Stream.
Wi' no soap nor no powder,
A wee dunk makes them clean.
It has great cleansing powers,
The Muttonburn Stream.

4.
And the ducks love to waddle there,
From morning till e'en.
Though they dirty the water, still
They make themselves clean.
And I've seen them at even, when
Their tails were scarce seen,
Waddling down in the muck
Of the Muttonburn Stream.

5.
Well, coming home from a party,
All gay and serene;
Sure they gave great parties
That lived round the Stream.
Coming home in the morn-time,
Not a light to be seen,
Sure I slipped and I fell in
That Muttonburn Stream.

THE PARTING GLASS

With Brendan Behan's 'Oul' Triangle' and the MacPeakes' 'Go, Lassie, Go' this is a first-rate song to lure an audience to loosen their inhibitions and sing out. The air is 'Sweet Cootehill Town'. What better reason to include it in our songs of the North of Ireland? Note too that it is warmly sung by our Scottish cousins, as I was delighted to find on a pleasant evening in Campbelltown, in the Mull of Kintyre at a singsong in 1967.

The Parting Glass

1.

Oh, all the money e'er I had
I spent it in good company;
And all the harm that I've e'er done,
Alas 'twas done to none but me.
And all I've done for want of wit
To memory now I can't recall;
So fill to me the parting glass,
Good night and God be with you all.

2.

If I had money enough to spend
And leisure time to stay awhile;
There is a fair maid in the town
Whose beauty does my heart beguile.
Her cherry cheeks and ruby lips
With magic hold my heart in thrall.
So fill to me the parting glass,
Good night and God be with you all.

3.

Oh, all the comrades e'er I had
Were sorry for my going away;
And all the sweethearts that I e'er had
Would wish me one more hour to stay.
But since it falls unto my lot
that I should rise and you should not;
I gently rise and I softly call,
Good night and God be with you all.

CHAPTER NINE

Carousing Songs

We have cast our net wide into Connacht, but still north of our line from Blacksod to Carlingford, to make room for this great drinking song; fit to stand alongside Fitzgerald's *Rubaiyat of Omar Khayyam*. Riocárd Bairéad will live for this gem of the eighteenth century, while glasses are raised and voices resound. If the *Rubaiyat* can be sung (?) with as much gusto as 'Preab san Ól' then Irish men should agree to masticate their tankards, come the end of a night's carousing; or should that be of nights'?

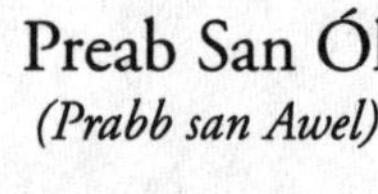

Preab San Ól

(Prabb san Awel)

BOOZING

1.

Siomaí sli sin a bíos ag daoine,
Ag cruinniú píosaí 's a' déanamh stóir.
Is a laighead a smaoiníos ar ghiorra'n tsaoil seo;
Is go mbeidh siad sínte faoi leac go fóill.
Más tíarna tíre, diúic nó rí thú;
Ní chuirfear pighinn leat is tú a' gabháil faoi fhód.
Mar sin is dá bhrí sin níl beart níos críonna,
Nó bheith go síorruí 'cur preab san ól.

Many are the ways that folk employ,
Gathering sovereigns, amassing wealth;
And how little they ponder on life's brief span,
And they'll stretch beneath the gravestone yet.
Be you a landlord, a duke, a king;
Not a penny goes with you beneath the sod.
And so, be sure, there's no better ploy,
Than ever and always to get royally drunk.

A blazing biblical reference, now.

2.

An ceannaí craosach níl meon nó slí ar bith
Le h-ór a dhéanamh nach bfeicthear dó.
An ráta is daoire ar an earradh is saoire,
Is ar luach sé phíghne chuirfeadh sé coróin.
Dá réir chaint Chríosta is ní dó-dhéanta
Le camall cíocrach a thabhairt tríd cró.
Mar sin is dá brí sin níl beart níos críonna,
Nó bheith go síorrui 'cur preab san ól.

The greedy merchant, there is simply no way
Of making money unknown to him.
His prices dearest, his goods cheapest,
For sixpenceworth he'll charge a crown.
By Christ's own words it's so hard a task
To squeeze a greedy camel through the needle's eye.
And so, be sure, there's no better ploy,
Than ever and always to get royally drunk.

Existentialists and hedonists alike might rise to the bait of this next verse. Apt biblical reference again.

3.

Is gearr an saol tá ag an lile sciamhach,
Cé gur geal is gur buí a gabháil.
Agus Solamh Críonna in a chulaith ríoúil,
Nach bhfuil baol air i n-áille dhó.
Ach níl sa tsaol seo ach mar sheinneán gaoithe,
Gá a scaoiltear nó slam de cheo.
Mar sin is da bhrí sin níl beart níos críonna,
Nó bheith go síorruí 'cur preab san ól.

How brief the life of the lovely lily,
However bright and yellow she goes.
And Solomon the Wise in his kingly robes,
Isn't his demise surely foretold?
Now what is life but a puff of wind,
A dart cast off; a handful of mist?
And so, be sure, there's no better ploy,
Than ever and always to get royally drunk.

FILL UP THE JAR

Seán Bán liked his sup, but these well-wrought verses speak for all, young and old, who warm to the juice of the barley. The weaving of the smooth vocables eases the dram on its downward path.

Flann O'Brien's 'Pint o' Plain is Your Only Man' is fine, but he must yield sway to Seán Bán here.

Líontar Dúinn An Crúiscín

(Leen-turr Doo-in Un Khroo-skene)

FILL UP THE JAR

1.

A bhuachaillí, a bhuachaillí molaim sibh go síorruí;
Sibh 'thógfadh croí na gcailín's chuirfeadh
gnaoí ar chruinniú daoine.
Nuair a smaoitím ar na scafairí 's iad
cruinn ar Ard an Aonaigh;
A' caochadh ar na streabhógaí
's a' cogarnaigh go síodúil.
Is líontar dhúinn a' crúiscín is bíodh sé lán.

Boys O boys O boys, I always admired you.
You surely amused the lassies
and put heart in any gathering.
When I recall the gallants,
all gathered on the Fair Hill;
Winking at the bonny ones
and whispering so smoothly;
So fill us up the crooskeen and keep it full!

2.

Isteach go tigh a' leanna libh a chailíní na dílse;
Braon de shú na bráich a chuirfeas
mothú in bhur gcroí istigh.
Ólfaimid is ceolfaimid is
beimíd seal go síamsach;
Beimid súgach meanmnach is pleoid
ar bhuaireamh 'n tsaoil seo.
Is líontar dhúinn a' cruiscín is bíodh sé lán.

All ye lovely maidens, all into the alehouse.
Have a sup of the malt-juice
to put life in heart's core.
We'll drink and we'll sing and
we'll have a heigho time;
We'll be merry, mettlesome;
to hell with life's cares.
So fill us up the crooskeen and keep it full!

3.

B'ann a bhiodh a' chuideachta
a' teacht 'na bhaile ó'n aonach.
A' gealghairi 's a priollaireacht 's a'
feiteamh le 'ar mian 'fhail.
Fá dheireadh théadh gach scafaire
'r ghreim sciatháin le na chaoimhbheart.
Sios a' mhalaí Raithní 's iad
a' portaíocht go croíúil
Is líontar dhúinn a' crúiscín is biodh sé lán.

All the merry company,
homing from the fair.
Joking and blethering,
seeking out our chance.
At length every buck goes off
arm-in-arm with his sweetheart;
Down the heather brae
whistling free and easy.
So fill us up the crooskeen and keep it full!

CATHAL BUÍ (TAWNY CHARLIE)

Two hundred or so years on, Tawny Charlie MacElgunn still lives fresh and vibrant, particuarly in his own Cavan, Monaghan and Fermanagh. 'You're Cathal Buí?' a priest asked. 'Aye, that's how ill-mannered folk style me.' A priest put him up for the night — after all if Cathal had not lifted his hand from the plough at the seminary in Salamanca, he'd have been one of them himself — to find the return for his fine supper and wine of the night before was to have his silver and plate plundered and gone the next morning.

Word came to that parish that the 'rogue' had died an edifying death.

'Edifying!'

'That fellow has as much chance of seeing heaven as I have of seeing this key,' casting it far out in the lake. That evening a local angler caught a fine trout. He sent it up to the priest. Key returned.

That 'edifying' death in a wretched fever-hut (typhus?), on the outskirts of a village. A poor little fire provided the charred twigs to scrawl his pitiful 'graffito', his *Aithreachas*, (remorseful *confiteor*) with its sonorous opening:

Anois is tráth liom parlaidh 'dhéanamh feasta le Dia.

(Now it behooves me to make my parley with God.)

The great nineteenth-century archbishop, John MacHale, said of Cathal that a man who made such an *Aithreachas* would find God's mercy.

One verse alone is a good prayer.

A Íosa, a Spiorad Naofa, a Athair is a Uain,
A thug fíor-fhuil do thaoibhe
d'ar gceannacht go cruaidh.
Bí 'mo dhídean; bí 'mo smuaintibh,
bí ar m'aire gach uair;
Má's suí dom, má's luí dom,
má 's seasamh, má's suan.

Jesus Holy Spirit, Father and Lamb;
Who gave your precious blood
to redeem us so hard.
Protect me, be in my thoughts,
watch over me at every hour.
Whether I sit or lie;
whether I stand or rest.

But what a piteous finale to all the carousing and wenching; to all the disregard of a tormented wife. And the echo of those seminarian days in Spain's Salamanca.

Sé mo mhilleadh go bhfuair mise léann an tsagairt ariamh.

(My woe that I was ever schooled to be a priest.)

One hard winter's morning, perhaps 'hungover' after a night's or even many nights' carousing, he came across a yellow bittern, lying stiff and cold; lost for a sip from the water of the frozen lake. His 'Buinneán Buí' will go down to posterity, as with Catullus's sparrow. So here is his elegy for the long-necked bittern with its booming cry.

An Buinneán Buí

(Ann Bwinnahn Bwee)

THE YELLOW BITTERN

1.

A bhuinneáin bhuí sé mo léan do luí,
Is do chnámha sínte tairéis do ghrinn.
Is chan easbhaí bí ach díobháil dí
A d'fhág do luí thú ar chúl do chinn.
Is measa liom féin na scrios na Traoi
Thú bheith do luí ar leacaibh lom
Is nach dtearn tú dith nó dolaidh sa tír;
Is nárbh fhearr leat fíon nó uisce poill.

My yellow bittern, I'm in pain for your fate;
With your bones stretched out after all your fun.
No dearth of food but the drink being scarce
Brought you to be lying here on your back.
It grieves me worse than the sack of Troy
That here you lie on uncaring stones.
And damn the harm or wrong you've done:
And you'd shrink from wine for a brackish pool.

2.

Nach buartha gránna fuair tú an bás,
A bhuinneáin áluinn a ba deise dreach;
Nach minic sa lá a rinne tú an grág
Ar shiúl go sámh fá gach tulaigh ghlas.
'Sé mo thuirse mór is m'ábhar bróin
Gur airde go mór do thóin ná do cheann.
'S gurab é deirfeadh gach pótaire a shiúlfadh an ród;
Go mbéitheá beo dá n-ólfa an leann.

What an ugly woesome fate your death,
My lovely bittern who ever looked fine.
All day long you'd croak away,
As you trotted serene on each grassy mound.
What bothers me and saddens me
Is here your ass is above your head.
And every boozer that walks the road
Knows a slug of beer would have saved your life.

3.

D'iarr mo stór orm leigean den ól,
Nó nach mbéinn-se beo ach seal beag gearr;
Sé duirt mé léi go dtearn sí an bhréag,
Nó gurbh' fuide do mo shaol an braon-so' fháil.
Nach bhfeiceann tusa éan an phiobáin réidh,
Go dteachaidh sé a dh'éag de'n tart ar ball?
Is a dhaoiní chléibh, fliuchaidh sibh mur mbéal,
Nó dan re braon 'fhaghas sibh i ndiaibh bhur mbáis.

My darling begged me to give up the drink,
Or all I'd live would be a little while.
I replied that that was surely a lie;
For my life would be longer for each drop I'd get.
Don't you see yon bird with his scrawny neck,
How thirst just lately has caused his death?
So all my pals, wet your thrapples well,
For damn the drop you'll get after your death.

CHAPTER TEN

A Little Merriment

The great Gaels of Ireland whom all the gods made mad;
For all their wars are merry and all their songs are sad.
[Chesterton.]
Some merry songs then.

THE KING'S GUARDSMEN
This piquant, mysterious little song baffles explanation; at least during the half-century and more since I first went and heard the incomparable Hughey Phaddy. His cousin, Conall Ó Dónaill, splendid singer too and consummate orator – my warm friend, still happily with us – ventures that the 'Guardsmen' were some local roustabouts, used in a facetious manner to point up the song. It does not ring true. Maybe a better explication is round some near corner.

Gardaí An Rí

(Garr-dee on Ree)

1.

Rachaidh mise suas le Gárdaí 'n Rí,
Agus bhéarfaidh mé anuas ar láimh liom í.
Nach mise chuirfeadh cluain ar a bán-chrios mín;
Agus bhéarfaidh mé go Tuadh Mhumhan í,
grá mo chroí.

I'm going up to the King's Guardsmen;
And I'll bring her back with me hand in hand.
I'm the boy to vanquish her lovely little waist;
And I'll take her down to Thomond,
my loved queen.

Curfá

Tógaidh í suas ar ghruaidh-mhín an iomaire;
Lasadh in a grua agus bua gach duine léi.
A ghiolla tá gan ghruaim, chuirfeadh cluain
ar an iomaití;
Nach é mo scéal trua gur luaíodh mise leat.

Chorus

Raise her up high on the edge of the ridge.
Her healthy, lovely cheeks and all in her thrall.
My guileless maiden fair, who'd lead lots of men astray.
What a hapless day for me
to have your name linked with mine.

2.

Níl mise tinn agus níl mé slán:
Ach is ró-mhór m'osna is ní fhéadaim a rá.
Nuair a smaoítim ar an uair údaigh
bhí me's tu, a ghrá,
Guala ar ghualainn is lámh ar láimh.

I'm not sick and I'm not well;
But my sighing is heavy and I don't know why.
When I think of yon time
when you and I, my dear,
Went shoulder to shoulder and hand in hand.

Curfá

Chorus

3.

Galar claoíte choích' a' grá;
Is mairg ar a mbíonn sé dh'oíche's lá.
Mar is crua an rud a snaídhm is
chá scaoiltear é go brách;
Is a chomrádaí dílis go dtéidh tú slán.

Love is a fever that can't be cured;
Woe to him who bears it night and day.
For its knot binds tight and
it never can be loosed;
And, my own dear comrade, may you fare well.

Curfá

Chorus

THE ISLE OF DOON RAWA

Another lovesong from Donegal. The melody resembles a fine drinking song from Ballymacoda in County Cork. I feel a special affinity here; I had a great-grandmother from Donegal, from Shroove, Moville, Annie Gillespie who married in September 1860 Edward O'Connor, a coastguard from County Cork. So my affection down the years for Counties Donegal and Cork. *'Torramh an Bhairille'*, 'The Wake of the Barrel', and *'Inis Dhún Rámha'*, 'Inishdoonrawa' are both great songs.

1.

'Rí na Cruinne gan mé's tú 'n-Iorras
no thiar i n-Inis Dhún Rámha;
Ar bhruach na Finne le taoibh na toinne
a' féachaint loingis thar sáile.
Dá mhéid ár dtuirse's gan aoinneach againn
ach géagán duilliúr ár sábháil;
Sé deirfeadh gach duine gur
lách ár n-imeacht mar d'éalaigh
Diarmuid le Gráinne.

O Lord of the Universe, that you and I might
be in Erris or west in Inishdoonrawa,
By the banks of the Finn, beside the sea,
viewing the ships go passing.
No matter how tired, all there on our own,
only the boskage for shelter.
All would declare that
our going was as grand as that
of Diarmuid and Gráinne.

2.

'Réir go bhfaca mé féin ann m'aisling,
mar bheadh sí ar bhacán mo láimhe;
'n spéirbhean mhaiseach mar aon bhrat sneachta,
dá mbeadh gan casgairt a dhéanamh.
Taobh na macnaidh dá mbiodh in m'aice,
mar chéile leapa gan airnéis.
'S é a béilín meala a léasfadh mo ghalar,
agus bhéarfadh mo cholainn 'un sláinte.

Last night I saw her as in a vision,
as if we were arm in arm.
This comely maid as dazzling as the snow-sheet,
before the thaw had come.
If I had that noble miss beside me,
my bedmate without a dowry,
Her honey-sweet mouth would
cure all my ills, and restore my body to full health.

3.

Dá mbínn mo bharrún ní dhéanfainn dabhar
ar spré bó, capall nó caorach.
Dá bhfaghainn-se 'n ainnir i na suí
le m'aice; nó í in a seasamh go haerach.
Tá gné ar a craiceann míl' uair níos taitmhí
ná éirí mhaiseach na gréine.
Is ní bréag a chanaim ach is fíor a n-abraim
gur b'í thug mais' ar gach maighdean.

If I were a Baron I wouldn't seek
a dowry of herds of steeds, cattle or sheep.
If only I won this damsel to sit by my side;
or to stand so pertly before me.
The bloom on her cheek is infinitely lovelier
than the gleaming sun at the dawn;
And never a lie do I tell but the truth,
that she far surpasses all maidens.

Tá Mo Chleamhnás á Dhéanamh

(Tah Muh Klow-nuss ah Yain-oo)

I'M FOR GETTING MARRIED

1.

Tá mo chleamhnas a dhéanamh inniu agus inné;
Is ní mó nó go dtaitníonn an bhean údaigh liom féin;
Ach fuígfidh mé 'mo dhiaidh í is rachaidh mé leat féin,
Fá bhruach na coille craobhaí.
Fá bhruach na coille craobhaí 'chonaíonn sí.
Tá 'n guth aici is binne nó 'n chuach is í a' glaoí;
Tá 'n coim aicí is gile nó 'n eala ar an tuinn.
Sí'n cailin deas bán a bhfuil mé 'ngrá leí.

Curfá

Shiúl mé thoir agus shiúl mé thiar;
Shiúl mise Corcaigh agus sráid' Bhaile Átha Cliath.
Macasamhail mo chailín níor casadh dom aríamh.
Sí an cailín deas bán a bhfuil mé i ngrá léi.

2.

Codladh go h-éadartha sea b'aite liom féin;
Leaba glas de luachair bheith faoí mo thaoibh.
Buidéal uisce bheatha bheith faoí mo cheann;
Is mo chailín deas bán bheith ar láimh liom.
D'éirigh mé ar maidin dhá uair roimh a' lá;
Agus scríobh mise litir ionnsair mo mhíle grá;
Go raibh a' londubh is a' smaolach
is na daoine 'ra;
Gur éalaigh sí uaim thar sáile.

Curfá

1.

I'm engaged and signed for yesterday and today;
and yon lady is far from pleased with me.
But I'm going to leave her and off I'll go with you,
by the edge of the branchy wood.
In that same branchy woodside, that's where she dwells.
Her winsome voice is sweeter far than any cuckoo's call.
Her slender waist is lovelier than the swan upon the wave.
She's the bonny fair girl and I love her.

Chorus

I've travelled east and I've travelled west;
I've travelled Dublin streets and Cork as well.
The likes of my lassie I've never met before.
She's the lovely fair girl, she's my own love.

2.

Sleeping in till milking time, that is my delight.
A green rushy bed helping my repose.
A big bottle of whiskey snug beneath my head;
And my own fair-haired lady by my hand there.
I rose up that morning two hours before dawn,
And wrote and sent a letter to my dearest love,
That blackbird and missel-thrush and everyone
could say
How you'd deserted overseas from me.

Chorus

Caitlín Óg

(Kahtch-leen Awg)

YOUNG CAITLÍN

1.

A Caitlín Óg is tú mo stór,
go deo ní mian liom scaradh leat.
Ar Shliabh an Fhíaigh gur chaith mé 'n oích',
mar i ndúil go mbéinn i gcleamhnas leat.

Caitlín Óg, oh you're my love;
I wish that I never should part from you.
On the Raven's Mount I spent the night,
still hoping that you'd wed with me.

Curfá

Is fál lá leir-ó, randai bhú!
A' gcuala sibh cúrsaí Chaitlín?
Dá mbéinn-se beo bliain nó dhó;
Go mbéinn-se ag ól le Caitlín.

Chorus

Sing fal la lero, randi voo;
have you heard any news of Caitlín?
If I survive a year or two;
well then I'll drink with Caitlín.

2.

Bhí Caitlín Óg a' siúl a' ród
nuair a casadh Dónall Dubh uirthí;
Leag sé í ar chúl a' chlaí,
agus bhain sé míle meaig aistí.

Caitlín Óg went up the road when
Dónal Dhu came up with her.
He heeled her over behind the hedge,
and tickled and tickled and tickled her.

Curfá

Chorus

3.

Dá mbéinn 'mo tháilliúr nó mo ghabha,
'mo ghréasaí bróg a b'aite liom;
Dh'ainneoin Éireann is dá bhfuil beo,
go gcuirfinn-se clóc' ar Chaitlín.

Were I a tailor or a smith,
a cobbler I would rather be.
And for all Ireland's wealth and weal,
I'd put a cloak on Caitlín.

Curfá

Chorus

4.

Bhí mé oích' mo shuí liom féin,
nuair a d'éirigh mé ionns ar na cailíní;
Níor shíl mé choích' go bhfuighinn a' tslí,
go tóin a' tí ionns ar Chaitlín.

One night I was left there on my own;
so off I went to the lassies-o;
I never thought I'd find my way,
to the rear of the house to Caitlín's.

Curfá

Chorus

A Mhuire is a Rí

(A Whirra iss a Ree)

O VIRGIN, O LORD

Strike up once more with a livesome melody, hyperbole rampant as he tells her the tales of love.

1.

A Mhuire 's a Rí gan orm na méara,
Bhuailfeadh port ar phíobaí ceoil;
Bhuailfinn port aoibhinn an taobh seo den tír,
Nach gcuala sibh' riamh a léithéid go fóill.
Níl cuach ar chrann nach rachadh 'un scaoill;
Níl giorraí i dtom nach bhfuígfeadh a saol.
Níl duine 'bhfuair bás nach n-éireodh slán,
Le h-aoibhneas mo mhálaí 'séideadh cheoil.

O Mary, O Lord that I had the fingers,
I'd strike up a jig on the musical pipes;
I'd strike such a sweet jig in this district here,
That never a one of you e'er heard the like.
No cuckoo on bough but he'd race far away.
No hare in the hedge but would run for his life.
No one that has died but would rise up in his health,
With the delight of my bagpipes sounding out song.

2.

Is buartha bocht imníoch chaith mise 'n geimhreadh,
Gorta 's ampla tharam go leor.
Cuid de mo mhuintir idir dhá chondae,
Cuid i bhFearmanach is cuid i dTír Eoghain.
Ach tiocfad ar ball le ruaiteacht an tsámhraidh;
Is buailfead go teann mo bhata 'r an bhórd.
Suífead i seomra is scairtfead ar dhram,
Sé deirfeas si liom, 'Cuir glaic ar an scorn.'

Worried and bothered I spent all the winter,
Hunger and want wherever I'd go.
Some of my folk away in two counties,
Some in Fermanagh, some in Tyrone.
But soon I will come in the red heat of summer;
And down I will crash my staff on the board.
I'll sit in the snug and I'll call for a dram,
She'll say to me, 'Catch it there by the neck.'

3.

Glórthaí gan suim a chuir sí 'mo chionn,
An bhean a dúirt liomsa go gceannóchainn bó.
Is gan fhios cé 'n poll a bhfuígfí í ann;
Is nach n-ólfainnse pionnta dá bainne go deo.
Tá bainne agus im go fairsing le roinnt,
Ag mná Mhín na gCuibhreann is mo bhean-sa gan deor.
Sí an bhean a bheas liom an bhean gheobhas roinnt,
Dá ngluaisfeadh sí liom ar fud an tsaoil mhóir.

Foolish enough whims she put in my head,
The woman who told me I should buy a cow.
And no knowing what hole she'd be found there yet;
And never a pint of her milk I'd drink.
But butter and milk in plenty I'd find,
With the Meenagivran lasses while my lass went dry.
So the woman I'll have is the one who has lots,
If she set off with me across the wide world.

Caoineadh na Mná Óige

(Kheenoo nah Mra Awig-yeh)

THE YOUNG WOMEN'S LAMENT

Mar thiocfadh ar bhoin no'r chaoirigh.
(As when dealing with sheep or cattle.)

For once a woman's song, scarce enough in our repertoire. Fine lively melody. The oft-told tale of old lecher and fine lusty girl, quite incompatible.

1.

Thios a' cois na farraige
atá mé féin 'mo chónaí.
A' síor-dhéanamh lionndubh
ó mhaidin go tráthnóna.
'S mé a' smaoíteadh ar mo stóirín
a bhí 'riamh 'caint liom.
Is ar chuala sibh mar seoladh mé
go h-óg a' déanamh m'aimhlis.

Down by the seashore, it's
there I have my dwelling;
It's there I'm found lamenting
from morning unto noon.
Still pining for my own true love
who always had a word for me.
Haven't you heard how ill-fate struck me,
so young I was, a fool?

2.

A Mhuire nach mé'n trua
is mé pósta ar a' sclábhuí;
Nach ligeann amach 'un Aifrinn mé
lá saor nó Dia Domhnaigh.
Nach dtéid go tí a' leanna liom
is nach n-ólfadh giní óir liom;
Is nach dteannfadh le n-a chroí mé
mar dhéanfadh an buachaill óg liom.

Oh, Mary, am I not forlorn
in wedlock with this 'keoghboy';
He never lets me out to Mass,
on Holy Day or Sunday.
He never takes me to the pub,
nor drinks a gold guinea with me;
Nor cuddles me in a heart's hug
like any likely youth would do.

3.

Pósadh go h-óg mé
mar gheall ar na puntaí;
Ar lán mo dhá láimh
nár shásaigh 'riamh m'intinn.
Is is trua nach dtig sé i reacht amach
mar thiocfadh ar bhoin nó'r chaoirigh
An té nach dtaitneodh a mhargadh leis
cead a sheoladh arís 'un aonaigh.

Young enough I married,
only for the sovereigns;
The full of my two hands
that never pleased my mind.
Alas that it has never been as
when dealing with cows or sheep;
If a body rued their bargain
they could send it back next fair.

CHAPTER ELEVEN

Saints and Scholars

DEUS MEUS ADIUVA ME

This little bilingual hymn is ascribed to Maol Íosa Ó Brolcháin, a monk with the great South Derry name of Bradley.

Maol=bald/tonsured.

Íosa=Jesus.

The year, in the monastery founded by Saint Colmcille at his beloved Derry of the Oakgroves, was 1086. The simple lyrics, done into modern Gaelic, are wedded to a melody composed, I believe, by a man who did herculean work to inculcate a love for what is best in our native song, the late Seán Óg Ó Tuama; a valued friend.

Deus Meus Adiuva Me

MY GOD, ASSIST ME

1.

Deus meus adiuva me.
Tabhair dom do shearc a Mhic dhíl Dé.
Tabhair dom do shearc a Mhic dhíl Dé.
Deus meus adiuva me.

My God assist me.
Give me your love, dear son of God.
Give me your love, dear son of God.
My God assist me.

2.

Domine da quod peto a Te.
Tabhair dom go dian a ghrian ghlán ghlé.
Tabhair dom go dián a ghrian ghlán ghlé.
Domine da quod peto a Te.

Lord, give what I seek of you.
Give me lavishly, bright gleaming sun.
Give me lavishly, bright gleaming sun.
Lord, give what I seek of you.

3.

Tuum amorem sicut vis.
Tabhair dom go tréan a dearfad arís.
Tabhair dom go tréan a dearfad arís.
Tuum amorem sicut vis.

That I might love you as you wish.
Give me powerfully, I say it again.
Give me powerfully, I say it again.
That I might love you as you wish.

4.

Domine, Domine exaudi me.
M'anam bheith lán le do ghrá, a Dhé.
M'anam bheith lán le do ghrá, a Dhé.
Domine, Domine exaudi me.

My Lord, my Lord hear me.
May my soul be filled with your love, my God.
May my soul be filled with your love, my God.
My Lord, my Lord hear me.

PRAISE SAINT BRIGID

Our next hymn, in praise of the greatest Irish woman saint, Brigid, has its place in our Northern affection. She was born in Kildare, but had a great monastery at Faughart, on the edge of the border between Louth and Armagh. We sing it each feast-day, 1 February; while *Crois Bhríde,* her cross of woven rushes, is freshly made and worn by all.

Gabhaim molta Bhríde,
Ionmhain í le hÉirinn.
Ionmhain le gach tír í
Molaimís go léir í.

Lochrann geal na Laighneach
Soilsiú feadh na tíre.
Ceann na mban ar míne,
Ceann ar óghaibh Éireann.

Tig an Gelmhreadh dian dubh;
Gearradh le na ghéire.
Ach ar Lá 'le Bríde,
Gar dúinn Earrach Éireann.

Let us praise Brigid.
Revered she is in Ireland.
Revered she is in every land.
Let all sound her praises.

Lantern bright in Leinster,
Shining throughout our land.
Gentlest of all women,
Best of Ireland's virgins.

Comes Winter black and fierce,
Cutting with its keenness.
But come Saint Brigid's Day
Near is Spring in Ireland.

THE SEVEN BEATITUDES OF THE VIRGIN MARY

The young girl, Sarah Sheáin, a whole long lifetime ago in the Donegal Gaeltacht of Rann na Feirste, was intrigued and then bored at the incessant Alleluias which grandmother tacked on to the family rosary 'trimmings' each night. Only years later when she and I heard it sung, in the 'Seven Joys of the Virgin Mary', in that same Gaeltacht, did we feel its beauty. Grandmother was the great *seanchaí*, Gráinne Phroinsíais. She had all the great songs, but like her equally renowned daughter, Sorcha Chonaill, although they could not sing the songs, they had them word-perfect as part of the story that enhanced each song.

Only after many years coming to Rann na Feirste, learning its songs, did this lovely hymn surface. Bawdy songs and deeply religious alike were kept from the stranger.

Seacht Súailcí Na Maighdine Muire

(Shacht Sooahlkee nah Mayjaneh Mwirra)

The Seven Beatitudes of the Virgin Mary

1.

An chéad súailce 'fuair an Mhaighdean Bheannaí, Nárbh í sin féin an tSúailce 'bhí mór? Súailce 'fuair sí ó na hAon Mhac uasal, Go dtug sí 'un tsaoil é i mbothán cró.	The first joy of the Blessed Virgin; Was it not indeed a mighty joy? The joy she found from her only great Son; That she bore Him in a lowly byre.
Loinneog	*Refrain*
Sé is beannaithe a hAon Mac óg. Sé is beannaithe Naomh Muire Óigh. Na seacht súailcí dá ndéarfá is amharc ar a h-éideadh; Go bhfuightheá go síorruí an Ghlóir.	Blessed be her only Son, so young. Blessed be Mary ever Virgin. Say the Seven Joys and behold her vesture That you might secure glory ever more.
Alléluia! Alléluia! Allélui! Allélui! Alléluia!	Alleluia! Alleluia! Allelui! Allelui! Alleluia!

2.

An dara súailce 'fuair a' Mhaighdean Bheannaí; Nárbh í sin féin a' tsúailce 'bhí mór? Súailce 'fuair sí ó n-a hAon Mhac Uasal, Nuair a shiúl Sé léi a' ród.	The second joy of the Blessed Virgin; Wasn't that indeed a mighty joy? The joy she found from her only great Son; That she travelled with Him along the road.
Loinneog	*Refrain*

3.

An tríú súailce 'fuair a' Mhaighdean Bheannaí; Nárbh í sin féin a' tsúailce 'bhí mór? Súailce 'fuair sí ó na h-Aon Mhac uasal; Go ndeachaidh Sé a' léamh A leabhair.	The third joy of the Blessed Virgin; Wasn't that indeed a mighty joy? The joy she found from her only great Son; That He'd gone by reading His book.
Loinneog	*Refrain*

4.

An ceathrú súailce 'fuair a' Mhaighdean Bheannaí; Nárbh í sin féin a' tsúailce bhí mór? Súailce 'fuair sí ó na hAon Mhac Uasal. Nuair a rinn' Sé den uisce beoir.	The fourth joy of the Blessed Virgin; Wasn't that indeed a mighty joy? The joy she found of her only great Son; When He turned the water into wine.
Loinneog	*Refrain*

5.

An cúigiú súailce 'fuair a' Mhaighdean Bheannaí; Nárbh í sin féin a' tsúailce bhí mór? Súailce 'fuair sí ó na hAon Mhac Uasal; Go dtearn Sé an marbh beo.	The fifth joy of the Blessed Virgin; Wasn't that indeed a blessed joy? The joy she found of her only great Son; When He made the dead to live.
Loinneog	*Refrain*

6.

An seiseú súailce 'fuair a' Mhaighdean Bheannaí;
Nárbh í sin féin a' tsúailce bhí mór?
Suailce 'fuair sí ó na hAon Mhac Uasal;
Nuair a shaor Se le n-A fhuil a' domhan.

The sixth joy of the Blessed Virgin;
Wasn't that indeed a mighty joy?
The joy she found of her only great Son;
When He redeemed the world with His blood.

Loinneog

Refrain

7.

'An seachtú súailce 'fuair a' Mhaighdean Bheannaí;
Nárbh í sin féin a' tsúailce bhí mór?
Súailce 'fuair sí ó na hAon Mhac Uasal;
Nuair a thóg Sé ar neamh í beo.

The seventh joy of the Blessed Virgin;
Wasn't that indeed a mighty joy?
The joy she found of her only great Son;
When He raised her to heaven alive.

Loinneog

Refrain

Beannacht Dé liom féin.
Beannacht Dé liom féin.
Beannacht Dé le gach duine ar a' tsaol seo;
A deirfeas na Seacht Súailcí.

God's blessing on me.
God's blessing on me.
God's blessing on everyone on earth,
Who will say these Seven Joys.

Alléluia! Alléluia!
Allélui! Allélui! Alléluia!

Alleluia! Alleluia!
Allelui! Allelui! Alleluia!

CHAPTER TWELVE

A Diadem from Donegal

SUMMER WILL COME

Donegal's version of a great song, much loved, widely known. Pastoral and sailor lover loses his girl.

1.

Oró, tiocfaidh an samhradh agus fásfaidh'n féar;
Agus tiocfaidh'n duilliúr glas ar bharr na gcraobh.
Tiocfaidh mo rún-searc le bánú 'n lae;
Agus buailfidh sí tiúin suas le cumha 'mo dhiaidh.

Oro, the summer will come and the grass will grow,
And the green leaves grow on every tree.
My own true love will come at the dawn of day,
And she'll strike up a tune in woe for me.

2.

Is óg is is óg a chuir mise dúil i ngreann,
Is bhéinn a' súgradh le mo rún ar fáill.
Is níl baile cuain ar bith dá ngluaisfinn ann,
Nach bhfuighinn maighdean óg dheas a shiúlfadh liom.

How young indeed that I first learnt to sport;
And I'd court with my dear at every chance.
There's never a port around that I'd put ashore,
But I'd get a fine young lass to walk with me.

3.

Scairt mé 'réir ag an doras thall,
Agus scairt mé 'rís a' raibh mo rún ar fáil.
Sé dúirt a mámai liom nach raibh sí ann,
Nó gur éalaigh sí 'réir leis a' bhuacaill donn.

I called last night at yonder door,
And I called again was my true love there.
Her mam it was who told me she was gone,
For she'd skipped last night with the brown-haired lad.

4.

Shiúl mé thoir agus shiúl mé thiar,
Shiúl mé Corcaigh 's sráid' Bhaile Átha Cliath.
Shiúl mé na bailte seo fá bhrón le bliain,
A' cuartú mo rún searc a bain díom mo chiall.

I travelled east and I travelled west,
I travelled Cork and Dublin's streets.
I travelled all these towns in woe this year,
Seeking my own true love who stole my wits.

5.

Mo bhrón ar an fharraige mar sí tá mór,
Sí tá 'gabháil idir mé is mo mhíle stór.
Siúlfaidh mé na bailte seo agus siúlfaidh mé 'n ród,
Ach dheamhan bean a phósfas mé nó go dtéim faoi fhód.

My woe on the sea for it is surely big,
It is lying between me and my own dear love.
I'll walk through all these towns, walk the road,
But damn the woman I'll wed till I'm 'neath the sod.

Coinligh Ghlas' An Fhómhair

(Khunn-lee Khlass on Owe-irr)

GREEN HARVEST STUBBLE

One of the loveliest 'slow airs' in the Donegal Gaeltacht; particularly popular in Rann na Feirste. Indubitably, 'Coinligh Ghlas' an Fhomhair', 'Moll Dubh a' Ghleanna' and, of course, 'Geaftaí Bhaile Atha Bui' are 'immortal melodies'.

As Derek Bell stands by the latter two, I must champion the former. This simple, beautiful love-song tells it all, effortlessly, as the Gaelic has it, *gan barrchleite amuigh no bunchleite istigh.* (Without a feather disturbed, upper or lower.)

1.

Ar choinligh ghlas an fhómhair, a stóirín,
gur dhearc me uaim.
Ba deas do chos i mbróigín is
ba ró-dheas do leagan siúil.
Do ghrua mar dhath na rósaí
is do chuirníní bhí fite dlúith.
Mo nuar gan sinn ár bpósadh ar
bórd loinge ag triall 'un siúil.

By the green harvest stubble, my darling,
I looked around on all to see.
How lovely your foot in your little shoe,
how lovelier still your graceful walk.
Your cheek the hue of the roses,
and your ringlets so braided, thick.
My woe that we are not to wed
on board a ship a-sailing west.

2.

Tá buachaillí na h-áite ag gártha
is ag éirí teann;
Agus lucht na gcocán ard a' déanmh
fáruis do mo chailín donn.
Dá ngluaisfeadh Rí na Spáinne
thar sáile is a shlóite cruinn;
Bhrúfainn féar is fásach is bhéinn
ar lámh le mo chailín donn.

The local boys are cheering,
cheering and getting tense;
And the high-hatted folk are making
a home for my nutbrown maid.
If the King of Spain came over,
across the foam with his mighty host;
I'd pound grass and bare ground
to be hand in hand with my own brown lass.

3.

Ceannacht buaibh ar aontaíbh
go mbéinn agus mo chailín donn,
Gluais gus tar a chéadsearc 'gus
go dtéidh muid thar Gaoth Bearra' nonn.
Go scarfar ó na chéile bláth
na gcraobh nó'n eala o'n tuinn;
Ní scarfar sinn ó chéile is níl
ach baois dhaoibh a chur 'mur gcionn.

Selling cows at the fairs I'd rather
be with my nutbrown girl;
Come on, we'll go, sweetheart, till across
Gweebarra we make our way.
Until they are parted, the bough's blossom
or the swan from the wave,
We will never be parted, and ye would be
quite naïve even to think of it.

4.

Chur me litir scríofa ionnsair
mo 'sweetheart' is casaoid ghéar.
Chuir sí chugam arís í go raibh
a croí istigh i lár mo chléibh,
Coim na h-eala ar míne
no'n síoda nó cluimh an éin;
Is trom an osna ním-se nuair a
smaoítim ar bheith a' scaradh léi.

I wrote and sent a letter
to my sweetheart with sore complaint.
She promptly replied that
her heart's love was truly mine.
As downy soft as the swan's waist,
as any silk or plumage of birds;
I heave a heavy sigh to think
that she and I should ever part.

THE DESERTED SOLDIER

A passionate girl's cry in the English lyrics to this same melody of the abandoned soldier, 'On Wednesday Morning', strikes that hyperbolic, wildly exaggerated note:

This one and that one may court him,
But if any one wins him but me,
Both daily and hourly I'd curse them,
That stole lovely Johnny from me.

Our warrior is of feebler stuff. Too often we hear in recent bloody conflicts did the missive from home or from some atrabilious neighbour, 'Dear John…,' bring the scalding tale. In the muck-packed trenches of the 1914-18 War the one release too often was to raise deliberately a head above the parapet to be promptly despatched. Our swain seeks solace in song.

An Saighdiúr Tréigthe

(An Ṣahy-jorr Traig-heh)

THE DESERTED SOLDIER

1.

Nuair a d'éirigh mé ar maidin Dia Céadaoin',
Níor choisrigh mé m'éadán fairíor;
Nó gur bheir mé ar an arm ba ghéire,
Agus chuir mé a bhéal le cloich líomh.

When I rose up on Wednesday morning,
I didn't sign my forehead, my woe;
But I caught up my sharpest bayonet,
And whetted its edge on the stone.

2.

Chaith mise díom mo chuid éadaí,
Agus mo chiall mhaith gur leig mé le gaoith;
Is nuair a chuala mé iomrá ar mo chéad-searc,
Gur steall mé an corr-mhéar ó 'n alt díom.

I cast away my uniform,
And my good sense let go with the wind,
And when I heard the gossip on my sweetheart,
I hacked my finger off at the joint.

3.

Is fada mo chosa gan bhróga,
Agus is fuide mo phócaí gan phighinn.
Is fada me ag ól le mná óga,
Ach níor ól mé ariamh deor le mo mhian.

Too long now I've gone barefoot,
Longer still my pockets are bare.
Too long now I've drunk with the lasses,
But never once have I drunk with my dear.

4.

Is fada mo chrá croí-se a dhéanamh,
Mo thuamba a bhreacadh le saor.
Agus mo chomhnair a tógail lá 'n Earraigh,
Agus na buachailli deasa 'gabháil faoi.

How long now my heart is tormented,
My tombstone by the mason is cut.
My coffin will be lifted on a Spring day,
While the handsome lads bear me away.

FAIRY LORE

'On Going to Dublin Town'

A zealous, quizzical but brilliant son of Cork city, Seán Óg Ó Tuama, brought this rare Munster version of one of our very great slow airs to my cherished friend of Rannafast, County Donegal, Hughie Devanney. In Seán Ó Baoill's apt phrase, Hughie was a tune-smith; he made his own of any tune he heard. I have known some who were not happy with this knack of the great singer. I am not one of them.

The song tells of a distracted husband on the way to Dublin. He is confronted by a strange young fair woman who questions him about his ailing wife. Slowly he is led to the revelation that this enquiring lady is the real wife. The one sick at home had been left by the fairies. Fairies in Donegal, for us? Or in Cork? In the 1950s in Pomeroy, Country Tyrone, a stout cattle-dealer, Paddy Daly, said: 'Master, as sure as Our Lord is in the Blessed Sacrament there's fairies!' And Jimmy Toal of the Square 'couldn't get a sleep at night with the boyos fisslin' under the bed'.

Ar Ghabháil Go Baile Átha Cliath Dom

(Air Ghull Guh Bwella Klee-ah Doo)

ON GOING TO DUBLIN TOWN

1.

Ar ghabháil go Baile Átha Cliath dom
a' chéad lá den tseachtain,
Casadh cailán óg orm 'dtug mé
mór-chíon dí 's taitneamh.
D'fhiafair mé 'nglóir chiúin dí,
'Cá gcónaíonn tú, 'shearc-rúin?'
'Is i dTuaifín 'tá mo lóistin
is m'áit chónaí le fada.'

On my way to Dublin town
on the first day of the week,
I met a young lass
who delighted my eye.
Softly I enquired,
'Where do you live, my darling?'
'In Tooafeen I dwell;
I've lived there this long time.'

2.

'Ceist agam féin ort ó 's tú
is deireannai 'd'fhág a' baile;
Caide mar tá do chéile,
nó'n féidir nach maireann?'
'Ó, tá sí tinn tréith-lag
i bhfiabhras na leapa,
Agus mise le trí ráithe
ag na liaibh a' mo chreachú.'

'May I ask you this since
you've lately left home?
How is your wife;
or could it be she is not alive?'
'O, she is weak and most feeble,
in a fever abed,
And me these nine months
by the doctors being fleeced.'

3.

'Cé'r mhiste duit féin é
dá dtéadh sí faoi thalamh?
Gheofá bean is spré léi;
dúiche shaor agus fearann.
Bheadh airgead i do phóca
agus ór buí le scabadh;
Agus maighre óg dheas le
bheith a' cóiriú do leapa.'

'Why should you care
if she were beneath the soil?
You'd get a dowried woman,
with free estate and land.
With money in your purse
and yellow gold to squander;
And a lovely young maiden
to pat down your pillow.'

4.

''Ainnir na ndual buí, ná
h-iarr thusa mo mhealladh,
Tá muirín lag óg orm is
ní h-áil liom á scabadh.
Ní bheidh airgead i mo phóca
nó ór buí le scabadh
Nó aon cailín óg le bheith
a' cóiriu mo leaba.'

'My beautiful fair one,
don't try to allure me.
I've a feeble young family,
I don't want to desert them.
I'll have no money in my purse,
no gold to squander,
Nor any young lassie
to smooth out my pillow.'

5.

'Dar brí na dtrí leabhar, mura
labhraíonn tú go ciúin liom:
Bheirfidh mé liom thú ins
na gleanntain ar uaigneas.
Bheirfidh mé liom thú
mar a chonaíonn an éanlaith;
Sé mo chreach go bhface mise 'n lá
go raibh clann agam féin leat.'

'By the solemn three books,
if you don't speak me fair,
I'll take you with me in
the loneliness of the glens.
I'll take you with me where
the birds make their nests,
And I'm damned that I saw
the day when I bore your brood.'

Má Théid Tú 'un Aonaigh

(Mah Hedge To unn Ainee)

IF YOU GO TO THE FAIR

1.

Má théid tú 'un aonaigh biodh	If you go to the fair have the sheep
a' chaora leat, a h-olann is a h-uan,	with you, her fleece and her lamb.
Má bhíonn tú díomhaoín biodh do	If you're single have your own choice
mhian leat i dtoiseach a' tslua.	in the front of all the throng.
Bí aoíbhiúil ceanúil caoiuil	Be pleasant, friendly, amiable
agus molfar as sin thú;	and you'll surely earn your praise.
Ní h-í an mhaoín 'bhearfas i dtír thú	It's not your fortune will favour you
is ná mealltar léí thú.	and don't be deceived by it.

2.

Ara, 'ansacht cé 'r bh' ansa leat	Arrah, my dearest, what other man
fear eile agat nó mé?	is dearer to you than me?
Is gur tú an planda beag a shantaigh	And you the little plant that I've desired
mé i dtoiseach mo lae.	from my earliest of days.
Thug mé fancy duit gan amhras	You were my fancy without doubting
mar bhí mé óg gan chéill.	as I was young with no sense;
Is focal cainte ná raibh sa duine údaí	And may anyone who speaks ill of me
a mholfadh duit ach mé.	be left speechless while they live.

This song is a great favourite; particularly so for this incident. The old seanchaí, *storyteller, Gráinne Phroinnsías, was on her death bed. Her daughter, also a renowned* seanchaí, *Sorcha Chonaill, was attending her mother after the priest had given the Last Rites.*

'A mhathair, 'bhfuil a dhath ar bith do bhuaireamh?'

(Mother, is there anything bothering you?)

Thiontaigh an tseanbhean agus chan sí: *(The old woman turned and sang:)*

3.

Ara, 'chéadsearc an féidir go	Arrah, my first love, can it be that
gcodlaíonn tu san oích'?	you sleep through the night?
'N'é 'ard nach léir duit na saíghde	And do you not sense the arrows
tá a' polladh i mo chroí?	that go piercing through my heart?
Tá ní éigin a' mo bhuaireamh	There is something bothering me
is an arraing a' mo chlaoí,	and the sharp pangs leave me whelmed,
Is mé ag éisteacht le h-éanacha	As I listen to the wee birds
na coille 'gabháil a luí.	in the woodside going to rest.

Agus fuair sí bás. *(Then she died.)*

No fault to the vignette that neither mother or daughter were singers. But they did have all the great songs and the rich lore that always went with them. So she murmured the quatrain. A lifetime's dealing with songs has taught me a salutary lesson: that often non-singers have a deeper appreciation of the subtleties and richness of great songs than have too many singers. Never more so than in these Gaeltacht homes, where a whole household of three generations — that of the noted seanchaí, *Micí Sheán Néill — would softly vocalise every syllable of each great slow air as it was being sung, although non-singers themselves. Their songs, sung in their hearts.*

THE POET'S DESOLATION

Near our finale now; a great song of the twentieth century; to be capped by possibly a greater one almost two centuries earlier. It was my privilege to sing this grave-lay by the resident *ollamh* (professor) of Coláiste Bhríde, Seán Bán Fheilimí Mac Gríanna, over his grave at his funeral. Poor Seán had foretold in another of his poems, *'Cluinfear mé ag caint as an uaigh.'* (My voice will be heard from the grave.)

So, on a bitterly cold March Sunday morning Seán was laid to rest with his folk in Annagry cemetery. Raidio na Gaeltachta broadcast the requiem and funeral ceremonies. During the graveside oration, his and my close friend, Iosef Ó Searcaigh, nudged me that I was to sing 'Cumha an Fhile'. As usual for me, I kept my eyes tight closed while singing. So I missed what the R. na G. presenter spotted; tears all around of course, as expected. But a great white gull soared slowly up from the scene. Transmigration?

A few years later I sang it again in Glasnevin Cemetery, Dublin.

A good friend, Cearúl Page, told me his ninety-year-old mother, Róisín, had asked him to get her 'wee singer' to sing 'Cumha an Fhile' at her funeral. I was honoured to bid her farewell in the language she and her late husband, Tomás, had loved almost inordinately, as I do. He had been head of the Translation Department, Dáil Éireann.

I measc Laochra Gael go raibh siad.

1.

Is cumhúil thíos fá bhruach na mara,
Is gruama 'n saol is mé liom féin.
Gan sólás croí, gan comhrá carad
'Thógfadh cian díom is mhúchfadh léan.
Go domhain san oích' is mór mo mhearadh,
'Dúil go gcluinfinn guth an éin.
Mo bhrón níl ann ach tuaim a' bharra,
Is uaigneas síor fá ghlinntí 'n aeir.

Desolate I stand by the strand of the sea,
Life all astray, I all alone.
No heartsome gleam, no friendly chat,
To lift my gloom, to chase my woe.
Late at night I'm so astray,
Straining to hear the bird's lone cry.
But alas, it's only the booming bar
And loneliness ever in the vales of the sky.

2.

Níl ceiliúr cuach, níl blátha geala,
Teacht an Earraigh ann mar bhíodh.
D'imigh an smaolach, d'imigh an eala,
Tháinig smoladh ar gach craoibh.
Tá mo chairde gaol go síor'na gcodladh,
Ins an tSeanbhaile, fairíor;
Agus mise fágtha fuar fann folamh,
Mar each gan srian a' treabhadh 'n tsaoil.

No cuckoo cry, no gladdening flowers,
When the spring comes round again.
Gone the song-thrush, gone the swans,
Decayed and withered every branch.
All my own kinfolk lie sleeping
in our old churchyard, my woe;
But lone, neglected, limp and empty,
Like an unyoked beast I go ploughing on.

3.

Ní fheicim bádaí 'gabháil a' barra;
Ní fheicim daoine 'muigh a' snámh.
Ní fheicim slóite Domhach Earraigh,
Síos fa'n Bhainsigh mar ba ghnách.
D'imigh an spóirt as Tóin a' Bhaile,
D'éag a' sean dream a bhi sámh.
Mo thrua 'na ndiaidh nach mór a' chaill é,
Iad bheith scártha uainn mar tá?

I see no boats now cross the bar;
No people about there swimming now.
No crowds throng on Springtime Sundays,
Down the Bannshay as of yore.
Gone is the sport from Tonawella
All the fine old folk, all gone.
I lament their going, don't we miss them,
Gone from us for evermore?

4.

Grá mo chroí na laethe fada,
Chaith mé sios fá bhruach na trá.
Seal ag imirt le mo mhada,
Seal a súgradh le mo ghrá
Seal gan ghruaim fá bhruach an easa,
Féachaint bradán ar a tsnámh
Is a Rí na nDúl nach mór a' chaill é
Iad bheith scartha uainn go brách.

4.

All my love, those lengthy warm days,
Once I spent down on the shore.
Whiles sporting with my dog,
While courting with my love.
Whiles at ease by the edge of the falls,
Spying as salmon made their leap.
And Father of all, what bitter loss
They all are gone for evermore.

TRAGEDY LONG AGO IN DONEGAL

Our final song, that always brings the Gaeltacht live and brimming to all of us who first fell under its spell in the 1930s. This one has stood the test of time. Thanks to it, of which the erudite Gaelic scholar, great teacher of our songs, Seán Óg Tuama, has said: 'Níl fhios ag na hUltaigh féin conas chomh mór is tá "An Chéad Mháirt 'E Fhómhar" ('Even Ulster folk themselves do not fully appreciate it'). My thanks to it for bringing Derek Bell and me together. Meeting him first in 1979 at the *Oireachtas* I was expatiating on the liberty the brilliant musician, Seán Ó Riada, had taken in altering categorically our greatest Donegal song, learnt by me in Rann na Feirste in 1936.

'Sing it till we see.'

'An chéad Mháirt 'e fhómhar ba bhrónach is ba thuirseach mo scéal...

... m'aigne do dhiaidh.'

Derek Bell the while fully as quickly as I sang jotting down the music. We meet in his hotel room soon after. He has me sing the entire song, making me repeat and repeat difficult passages until he is satisfied. Incidentally, he refuted me much later for my iconoclasm, my scathing faulting of Ó Riada.

'Can you sing what Ó Riada left?'

'Oh, yes.'

'Then, that was all right.'

THE FIRST HARVEST TUESDAY

This song written in 1811 will live in the Donegal Gaeltacht, particularly in Rann na Feirste, while the language lives. Made by one of seven poet brothers, Séamus Ó Dónaill, it has won him the palm even over two better poets, his brothers Aodh and Pádraig. They never suffered the tragedy of losing his son, Pádraig. Father and son had paddled their flimsy currach across the narrow estuary of the Dobhar for a sack of meal to make a run of póitín. Coming back was the problem: two grown men, a heavy sack. The father set off the long road by land. Pádraig would be across hours before him. He wasn't.

'He's not here yet?'

'No.'

'He won't be so.'

Some time after the funeral the father was missing. They found him wandering by the steep slopes above the shore, where the tragedy occurred. He was singing. Aodh prophesied that Séamus's lament would be remembered long after their songs had slipped into oblivion.

An Chéad Mháirt 'e Fhómhar

(An Khaid Whart eh Ohwar)

THE FIRST HARVEST TUESDAY

1.

An chéad Mháirt 'e Fhómhar ba bhrónach
tuirseach mo scéal,
Lámh thapaidh bhí cróga ag dul romham
ar leaba na n-éag.
Ar Charraig na nDeor is dóigh
gur chaill mé mo radharc;
Is go dtéidh mé faoi fhód
ni thógfad m'aigne do dhiaidh.

On the first Harvest Tuesday
how weary, sad my tale.
That stalwart active arm going ahead of me
on that bed of death.
On the Rock of Tears I surely
have lost my sight;
And till I sink 'neath the sod
I'll not raise my mind in your wake.

2.

Tá do mháthair is Níall faoi chian
is is fada leo an lá;
D'fhág tú osna in a gclíabh nach
léigheasfadh dochtúir nó lia.
Ar a sholáthair mé 'riamh agus
biodh sé uilig cruinn in mo láimh;
Go dtabhairfinn é uaim ach
fuascladh – Pádaí bheith slán.

Your mother and Niall are distraught
through the wearisome day.
You left a sighing in their breasts
that no surgeon nor leech could cure.
If all I ever earned I had it gathered
now in the palm of my hand,
I'd cast it away to have
Paddy rescued and safe.

3.

Tá do deirfiuracha cráite de ghnáth
's iad a' sileadh na súl;
Is gan fhios cé'n lá go brách
a n-imeoidh a gcumha.
D'fhág tú d'aicme faoi smál 's nach
náir liom mar rinne tu a' siúl;
Nuair nár agair tú Párrthas le
spás beag eile 'thabhairt duinn.

3.

Your sisters are aghast each day
as they bitterly weep;
And who knows if ever their woe,
if ever 'twill cease.
You left all your kin tainted,
and I'm shamed that you slipped away;
That you didn't beg Paradise
to give us another wee while.

4.

Ba charthanach fial thú riamh
is ba sona do lámh;
Agus bheitheá faoi chian mur
ríartha dá dtiocfadh 'n do dháil.
Ba deismir do chiall le 'ach aon
de d'aicme ar a' tsráid;
's ní mhairfead beo bliain
i mbuaidhreadh in d'easbhuí mar 'tá.

Generous and kind ever
and how lucky your hand;
And you'd be sorely grieved if you hadn't
something for all that you'd meet.
Your wise word of sense
for any kinsfolk on the street;
And I'll not last a year in my woe,
in my loss that you're gone.

5.

Mo mhallacht go buan
faoi bhruach a' chladaigh seo thíos;
'S é d'fhág d'aicme faoi ghruaim is rinn
'gual dom in aice mo chroí.
'S é do chur ins an uaigh, monuar,
a d'fhág mise gan bhrí;
Gan mhisneach, gan stuaim ach 'mo
thruaill bhocht ag imeacht le gaoith.

My everlasting curse I cast
on that strand below;
It left your kinsfolk in grief and
a black coal in place of my heart.
With you laid in the grave,
alas, I'm left all astray;
No spunk, no wits, just an empty
sheath blown in the wind.

ENVOI

So now we have come full circle from the O'Donnell brothers in 1811, all of them poets, to their direct descendants, the Ó Gríanna brothers: Seosamh, pellucid prose writer; Séamus, almost his peer as novelist and short story writer, and facile song lyricist; and Seán Bán, whose 'Cumha an Fhile' will be sung in the next century as will 'An Chéad Mháirt 'e Fhómhar' in its third century. Ranging far and wide, from Antrim's Glens to the poets of South Armagh; from Cathal Buí's Cavan and Riocárd Bairéad's Mayo and to whose 'Carn tSíail'? On from them to the present-day vernacular in Tyrone and South Derry; along the shores of Lough Neagh; to Sliabh Gallen and Ligoniel Hill. From eighteenth-century masters to present-day upholders of a vibrant oral tradition in Irish and English, we have called these: 'traditional songs of the North of Ireland'.

Sing and be glad.
Slán agus beannacht.
So, now you have it from Derek and me. We feel no diminution of our treasury. Perhaps you may not have partaken of the bounty. If so, we have a Gaelic saying for you.

Mo thri thrua naoi n-uaire thu. (You're to be commiserated over and over again.) I am positive that Derek Bell, as is his wont, has noted down the melodies quite meticulously. I am happy that these songs that I love will get the hearing they merit.

If you, reader, are a singer, do sing these melodies. If you have the Gaelic then have a go; but much preferably hear a good traditional Gaeltacht singer. The saying goes: 'It cannot be taught, but it may be learnt.' If you are not a singer, not even in the bathroom, take heart. Our translations, never meant to be poetic renderings, are merely given as an indication of the meaning and flow of the lyrics.

Liam Ó Conchubhair agus Derek Bell. 1999.